The 1990s opened with the majority of its locomotives and rolling stock dating from the 1960s although liveries were on the [...] corporate stagnation. The scene is Scarborough in 1990 where an Intercity liveried Class 47 is in charge of an [...] still carries blue and grey. Lurking in the background is that 1980s invention the Pacer. It might have been ex[...] by the end of the decade but as this publication illustrates they remained to provide services into the 21st cent[...]

INTRODUCTION

Some dates in the evolution of our rail system come to mind easily, the Grouping in 1923, Nationalisation in 1948 and the Beeching report of 1963 being of particular importance. Perhaps few would see the events of the 1990s in that light, possibly because it was a process lasting much of the decade, but the '90s arguably saw the greatest change of all in our rail system with privatisation, booming passenger numbers and the arrival of locomotives that were not built in the UK. This publication traces those events in detail year by year.

Much of the information used in this publication was sourced from publications of the time and in particular *The Railway Observer*, the house magazine of the Railway Correspondence and Travel Society www.rcts.org.uk ■

CONTENTS

4	1990s Overview	58	1995
6	1990	66	1996
20	1991	78	1997
30	1992	86	1998
38	1993	98	1999
46	1994	106	1990s Railtours

COVER PICTURES

The old order is in charge. Class 101 DMUs were already well over thirty years of age at the start of the 1990s. This set stands at Clapham Junction in 1990 providing a service to Kensington Olympia, one that would change to electric traction before being extended to Willesden and DMU operation once more. T Owen/Colour-Rail

The new order cometh – a privatised railway running locomotives not built in this country. New Class 66s 66003/4/5 pose at Toton depot on August 29, 1998. Colour-Rail.com

ISBN: 978 1 80282 712 5
Editor: Paul Chancellor

Senior editor, specials: Carol Randall
Email: carol.randall@keypublishing.com
Design: SJmagic DESIGN SERVICES, India
Cover design: Daniel Jarman
Advertising Sales Manager: Brodie Baxter
Email: brodie.baxter@keypublishing.com
Tel: 01780 755131
Advertising Production: Debi McGowan
Email: debi.mcgowan@keypublishing.com

SUBSCRIPTION/MAIL ORDER
Key Publishing Ltd, PO Box 300, Stamford, Lincs, PE9 1NA
Tel: 01780 480404
Subscriptions email: subs@keypublishing.com

Mail Order email: orders@keypublishing.com
Website: www.keypublishing.com/shop

PUBLISHING
Group CEO: Adrian Cox
Publisher, Books and Bookazines: Jonathan Jackson
Head of Marketing: Shaun Binnington
Published by
Key Publishing Ltd, PO Box 100, Stamford, Lincs, PE9 1XQ
Tel: 01780 755131 **Website:** www.keypublishing.com

PRINTING
Precision Colour Printing Ltd, Haldane, Halesfield 1, Telford, Shropshire. TF7 4QQ

DISTRIBUTION
Seymour Distribution Ltd, 2 Poultry Avenue, London, EC1A 9PU
Enquiries Line: 02074 294000.

We are unable to guarantee the bonafides of any of our advertisers. Readers are strongly recommended to take their own precautions before parting with any information or item of value, including, but not limited to money, manuscripts, photographs, or personal information in response to any advertisements within this publication.

© Key Publishing Ltd 2023
All rights reserved. No part of this magazine may be reproduced or transmitted in any form by any means, electronic or mechanical, including photocopying, recording or by any information storage and retrieval system, without prior permission in writing from the copyright owner. Multiple copying of the contents of the magazine without prior written approval is not permitted.

Britain's Railways in the 1990s

INTRODUCTION

THE 1990s: POLITICS KEEPS PRIVATISATION FIRMLY ON TRACK

Before exploring the major rail events of the 1990s it is important to set them in the context of the 1990s in general.

Politics had always had an influence on what happened on our railways. Nowhere was that more evident than in the Labour Party inspired nationalisation of the system in 1948, although that was in part almost necessitated by the parlous state of the railways following World War Two. The start of the '90s saw the country sliding into an economic downturn, but also in the middle of many years of Conservative rule, long enough for them to implement some of their underlying beliefs such as privatisation. A number of industries had already been taken to the stock market and indeed the railways were left almost until last due to the difficulties in selling off what was at the time the county's largest company. As this publication explains the end result was to be a myriad of franchised passenger train operators, two freight companies and Railtrack looking after all of the infrastructure. The final stages of the process were rushed due to an impending General Election which the Tories lost with Tony Blair becoming Prime Minister on May 1,1997, by which time the economy was very much on the 'up' again. While Labour did not at that time seek to undo the basic structure of what the Tories had put in place, re-organisation to give the Government a greater element of control was soon on the agenda.

More widely on matters political, the early years of the decade saw continuing threats and indeed bombings connected to the situation in Northern Ireland with the IRA campaign being brought to the streets of the mainland with a particular emphasis on locations in and around the capital. The Good Friday agreement of 1998 finally saw an end to mainland bombings associated with Irish politics. That year also saw the establishment of the Welsh Parliament and the first election and meeting of the Scottish parliament took place in 1999. Also in the early '90s the police were having to deal with civil unrest. There was rioting, mainly in protest about the new Poll Tax that Prime Minister Margaret Thatcher had sought to impose. The early years of the decade also saw quite a deep financial recession with many redundancies and high levels of unemployment.

The country was part of the European Union, created as such in 1991, throughout the decade, but the Government decided that it would not introduce the new Euro currency that was launched on January 1, 1999.

Much of the bus industry went into private ownership in the 1980s, but London Transport buses had remained in public ownership (having split it into a number of operating companies) and the Government started that sell off in 1994.

Rolls-Royce sold off

Another transport change saw the last FX4 design of London cab produced in 1997. 1998 saw the car brand name Rolls-Royce sold to the Germans while Vauxhall Motors produced the first Astra. A social reform saw the introduction of vouchers for free nursery schooling for four year olds and the minimum wage, set at £3.60 for over 21s, was introduced in 1999.

In 1990 Liverpool, Manchester United and Nottingham Forest (managed by Brian Clough) were the leading football teams. It was a year of controversy when Swindon Town gained promotion to the first division only to be found guilty of financial irregularities with the punishment being relegation to the Third Division. After demonstrations by fans they were eventually allowed to remain in the Second Division. 1992 saw the establishment of the Premier League. England's hopes of playing in the World Cup in 1994 ended when they failed to qualify for the

Contrasting old and new- the frontage of Paddington tube station remained as it had been for most of the 20th century but the retail premises and pavement clutter represented the current day. A flower shop, a book makers and a Bureau de Change are the background to a display of tourist post cards, a plastic rubbish bin and bags and a modern bus shelter. The car is of German origin illustrating the decline of the UK based industry that built the likes of the Ford Sierra, a 1990s staple. D Pye Colour-Rail.com

4 Britain's Railways in the 1990s

1990s

London joined the rest of the country when London Transport buses were privatised in the middle of the decade. Whilst buses had to remain at least partly in LT red operators could add their own branding. As seen here the only clue to it being a London bus were two stickers carrying the LT roundel. As well as new liveries, vehicle standardisation also went out of the window. Here we see a Denis Dart with Wright bodywork, two manufacturers that would not have ever been thought of as providers of London buses just a few years earlier. Colour-Rail.com

final 32. Unsurprisingly, the team also failed to reach the final of the European 96 competition after a penalty shootout with Germany.

Motorway building was still under way although winding down from the levels of activity seen previously with the M20 and M40 completed. Damon Hill, the well-known racing driver received a seven day driving ban after being caught doing 165mph on the latter Motorway. One of the worst motorway accidents occurred in thick fog on the M42 in 1996 with three killed and 60 injured. It took one week to clear the wreckage.

In her Queen's Speech of 1992, Queen Elizabeth ll described the previous 12 months as a personal 'annis horribilis' (terrible year) with marriage difficulties and scandals besetting three of her children and a fire at Windsor Castle rounding off the period. However, the year paled into insignificance compared to the events surrounding the death of Princess Diana in 1997.

As well as the rioting seen in 1990/1, much racial tension remained with the murder of Stephen Lawrence in 1993. The teenager's death prompted decades of investigation into unrest in multi-cultural communities.

Much as today, the National Health Service was under pressure and the waiting list for treatment topped one million for the first time in 1993.

Two of the country's most notorious murderers made the headlines in 1994. 'Moors murderer' Mira Hindley was told she would never be released from prison and Fred West was charged with the series of murders in Gloucestershire. He was found dead in his prison cell on January 1,1995. One of England's most prolific killers, Dr Harold Shipman, was brought to justice in 1999.

March 1999 was a sad month for show business with the deaths of Dusty Springfield, Eric Morecambe and Rod Hull of Emu fame. Television journalist Jill Dando was murdered in April.

In the world of technology the mobile phone came into general use as it shrunk in size, but the internet - as we know it - only started life in 1990 becoming available for public use the year after. From three million users worldwide in its first year, it grew to 10 million in 1996 and 130 million in 1998. Ebay went live in 1995 and Google three years later.

Britpop was the general name given in the 1990s to a new wave of successful British bands who made a big impact abroad as well as in this country. The most successful groups were Radiohead, Oasis, Blur, Pulp, Massive Attack and the Spice Girls.

In fashion, puffer (quilted) jackets, the Wonderbra, body piercing, and T-shirts covered in slogans were some of the 'cool trends' to follow.

Operation Desert Storm in Iraq was launched in 1991, the same year in which Boris Yeltsin became the first elected leader of Russia and the following year Bill Clinton was voted in as the 42nd President of the USA

From 1990-1995 many in the UK were impacted by an end to the boom in property prices. House prices suffered sharp falls, particularly in southern Britain, and many were left in negative equity.

The decade ended with the opening of the London Eye on New Year's Eve. ■

The fashion trends of the '90s were not easy to spot when people wore coats more frequently, but as can be seen jeans were firmly established as a 'everyday' wear. This scene is taken at Middlesbrough station where the original ticket office had been retained during a station upgrade that saw lighter and brighter environments created complete with the obligatory ticket machine. P Chancellor/Colour-Rail.com

Britain's Railways in the 1990s

DECADE OVERVIEW
ALL CHANGE AS CHANNEL TUNNEL LINK BECKONS

Few outside the railway industry, and probably many within, had any inkling about the major changes that would be seen in the 1990s across British Rail.

The later 1980s had seen a strong growth in passenger numbers, reversing a decline that had been ongoing for decades and had also seen the start of the demise of the 'BR Blue' era where corporate colours and conformity had been the order of the day. Sectorisation was now in vogue in both the freight and passenger arenas this being the prelude to the privatisation programme that would be unleashed as the decade progressed. An early development in the decade was the formal creation of Regional Railways in November 1990, this having five operating areas and replacing the Provincial sector in providing all passenger services except for Intercity and the Network South East (NSE) area.

Investment in new passenger motive power had been minimal since the end of the 1960s until the arrival of the high-speed trains (HSTs) in the mid-1970s which by 1990 had revolutionised many Inter City journeys. The end of the 1980s saw the delivery of most of the class '90s, bolstering the West Coast fleet while the East Coast was about to become a fully electrified route for which the class 91 locomotives

British Railways blue reigned supreme from the end of the 1960s until the mid-1980s. Typifying those times is this picture taken at Glasgow Queen Street of Class 27 5367, so predating the application of a TOPS number, complete with a rake of blue and grey liveried stock on September 5 1972. Colour-Rail.com

1990s

The earliest of the DMUs numbered in the 5XXXX series were well over 30 years old at the start of the 1990s and there was an expectation at that time that they would very soon be a thing of the past, but some evaded the call of the scrap yard to see in the 21st century. However this Class 104 unit was on borrowed time but was typical of the breed still employed almost throughout the country as the 1990s dawned and is seen at Betws-y-Coed on September 9 1989. Colour-Rail.com

and Mk IV carriages were in the process of delivery which in turn would release some HST sets to bring about further improvements elsewhere. With money tight in the early 1980s the railways had invested in the supposed 'stop gap' Pacers, nominally for local and branch line duties, but their use on long distance duties had become common place. More robust diesel multiple unit (DMU) type deliveries had seen first the arrival of class 150s followed by 155 and 156 types. There should have also been a substantial fleet of Class 158 units operating by the end of the '80s but the first units were just being seen on test by the end of 1989. These units were intended to replace many of the services that had moved from being worked by first-generation DMUs to loco haulage, which was keeping many now aging locomotives employed on short formation passenger workings in many parts of the country. There were also still many first-generation DMUs – of at least 30 years of age – rattling their way across the countryside. Electrification of the East Coast mainline was a major undertaking and there was little activity elsewhere on such projects, the exceptions being the route between Portsmouth and Southampton which was still home to the equally ancient Thumpers of classes 205 to 207. There was an approval for the line from Carstairs to Edinburgh to be so equipped. The Portsmouth scheme went live from May 14.

Freight by rail was not so fortunate as the passenger sector in maintaining and growing volumes moved. Traditional industries such as coal and steel-making continued to decline while the installation of pipe lines had already reduced oil transport by rail. That said, the way in which goods moved around the world, and the growing tendency for many products to be sourced from distant lands, saw a growth in containerisation. As far as the UK rail scene was concerned this saw a constant increase in such traffic and although a number of ports dealt with containers, Felixstowe gained a pre-eminent position. This posed an increasing challenge due to the fully stretched single line that served the port from Ipswich.

As mentioned above, the industry relied very much on locomotives built in the 1960s, the more recently constructed heavy freight types, classes 56 and 58 numbering only some 185 out of a diesel loco fleet which at the start of the decade totalled around 1900 compared with numbers approaching 6000 at their peak. All of the older classes were seeing members withdrawn including the Class 50s, these being the last to be built prior to the arrival of Class 56. Due imminently but seriously delayed was the order for 100 Class 60s. These powerful machines were intended to haul heavier trains, thus increasing payload but in theory at least, reducing the number of services required. Alternatively, the number of trains could remain the same but allow a growth in tonnage moved by rail to be achieved. The electric loco fleet would peak at around 290 units before the removal from stock of classes 81 and 85, these being the last of the types delivered in the early 1960s. It should be noted in respect of what transpired in the 1990s that privately owned diesels authorised to run on British Railways at the start of 1990 totalled just seven being two Class 20/9 for weed killing duties and five Class 59s working the Mendip stone trains. No heritage diesels were allowed to operate on the network.

In hindsight it is interesting to see how policies changed over the years, particularly in respect of the naming of locomotives. At the outset of the modern traction programme naming of front line locomotives was still 'the thing to do' and the early English Electric Type 4s, all of the Western Region Type 4 hydraulics and the Deltics carried names. Plans to extend naming to e.g. some Class 37s however foundered with plates that had been fitted and covered over, then being removed without ever being seen by the public. The Western region managed to name a handful of Class 47s but thereafter the practice of naming engines ceased and remained 'forbiddden' for a number of years. The start of the 1980s brought about a

7

The fastest growing port handling containerised goods was Felixstowe. The port complex itself was relatively easily expanded, but the same could not be said of the mainly single track branch to Ipswich, the capacity of which became a major problem during the '90s. Here we see the southern freightliner terminal at the port in 1981. Colour-Rail.com

revival in namings with the GW 150 celebrations even seeing some named engines being turned out in pseudo GWR liveries. Names became increasingly diverse, and perhaps a mystery to the public in some cases, as locos were named after everything from places to important customers of the freight industry. Although most of these names were applied 'officially' with cast plates, motive power depots started painting local names on shunters and Tinsley depot embarked on a naming programme for its Class 47s. Thus it was by the start of the 1990s names were going onto and coming off locos with great regularity and increasingly also the HST fleet.

The Channel Tunnel was the major construction project of the time, although it was yet to be decided how trains through the tunnel would reach London, and as mentioned above, completion of the East Coast electrification programme was another. Despite the route to London not being finalised it had been decided that Waterloo would be the International terminal, requiring

Some of the first chinks in the armour of standard liveries were to be found on the Western region where Great Western green was applied to some Class 47s, ostensibly to celebrate the Great Western 150 event of 1985. One such was 47484 seen at Cockwood Harbour on July 16, 1989 by which time the days of blue and grey express passenger stock were numbered and a couple of Intercity liveried carriages have been inserted into the formation. Colour-Rail.com

Britain's Railways in the 1990s

1990s

much construction work to be undertake, this of course impacting on the always harassed daily commuters. However formal approval was only given in the spring with completion scheduled for early 1993. Late 1989 saw the placing of an order for the rolling stock to operate Channel tunnel passenger services. At an estimated cost of £500m, 30 300kph train sets were specified comprising of two locomotives with eighteen articulated carriages between each. Ownership of the sets was to be split between BR (14) SNCF (13) and SNCB (3). As well as having shared ownership, companies involved in the construction were also from the UK, France and Belgium with the first sets due for delivery in 1992. At the time it was intended that services would run beyond London with for instance services from Wolverhampton to Paris and Brussels. Approved subsequently was an order for twenty high powered electric locomotives designated as Class 92. Also related to the project was the electrification of the Redhill-Tonbridge line to provide a second route that could be used by trains planned to run through to destinations other than London. Completing a spend of £250m was the go-ahead to build a depot at North Pole for stock maintenance.

Despite these two major projects the overall theme was one of continued rationalisation of facilities, although most comprised the removal of a set of points here and a small yard closure there. With the demise of wagon load freight there was little need for marshalling yards and the major hump yards of the '60s and '70s had either been closed down or remained as just a set of often weed infested sidings.

Those commuting through Britain's busiest railway station at the start of the 1990s had to endure many months of construction work at the site to build Waterloo International station to accommodate the arrival of Channel Tunnel services. Work is seen in progress on March 13, 1991. T Owen/Colour-Rail.com

The heritage sector however was enjoying buoyant times both with steam specials on network routes and was supported by a plethora of preservations schemes across the country. The major lines were becoming viewed as tourist attractions rather than a place where enthusiast played trains and were growing as a source of employment opportunities as paid staff took on the role of day to day management. Nonetheless, a number of the lines ran over only parts of the routes we know today and so the decade witnessed the continued growth of the sector. ■

The earliest of the electric loco classes used on the West Coast mainline were more than 30 years old at the start of the '90s. Classes 82-84 had already departed the scene and 81s and 85s would soon suffer a similar fate, but on July 4, 1987, 81011 approached Crewe with what today would be termed an Intermodal train, the movement of containers by rail having become the fastest growing freight sector in the industry. D Pye/Colour-Rail.com

As part of the upgrading of the Chiltern lines project a new depot was to be built at Aylesbury thus rendering the facilities at Marylebone redundant, The depot there is seen in 1983. Colour-Rail.com

1990

SPEED AND PRESERVATION

Although privatisation of the railways was seen to be on the political agenda, many enthusiasts did not associate what seemed to be frequent organisational changes with what became 'the elephant in the room'. The year saw the setting up of 'Areas' within Network South East and two were created: Great Eastern, essentially the line from Liverpool Street to Norwich and lines east, and West Anglia covered lines westward to its boundary with the East Coast mainline.

Upgrading of the Chiltern route was under way with line speeds being raised to 75mph in a number of places which, along with the new units due in 1991, would see Banbury-Marylebone journey times cut by 17 minutes. Remodelling at Marylebone saw the station reduced to four platforms, all under the overall roof. Marylebone diesel depot was to close, being replaced by a new depot at Aylesbury. NSE also had a new depot opened at Reading late in 1990 where other improvements on the line to Paddington were expected to reduce commuting time by fifteen minutes.

A new initiative was the formation of the company Charterail in which BR had a 22% interest with the company acting as a distribution contractor including road haulage, mainly using Road-Railer and Tiphook's 'piggyback' concepts, with rail providing the long distance mode on a sub contract basis.

In another change BR introduced new livery rules for rail tankers conveying hazardous liquids where certain colours of band applied to the tank body would denote the type of liquid carried, this being in addition to the standard hazard labelling.

In recent years much has been made about the vulnerability of the sea wall at Dawlish but washouts and damage there are nothing new. There had already been damage events in the 1980s and in December 1989 major damage was once again caused to the wall and during January 1990 extensive repair work was undertaken although mainly at night to prevent disruption to services. Emergency work at the time of the washout only caused a two day suspension of services. Another sea wall giving problems was that at Towyn between Rhyl and Abergele which was breached on February 26 causing North Wales coast services to be suspended for one week. With BR being responsible for the maintenance

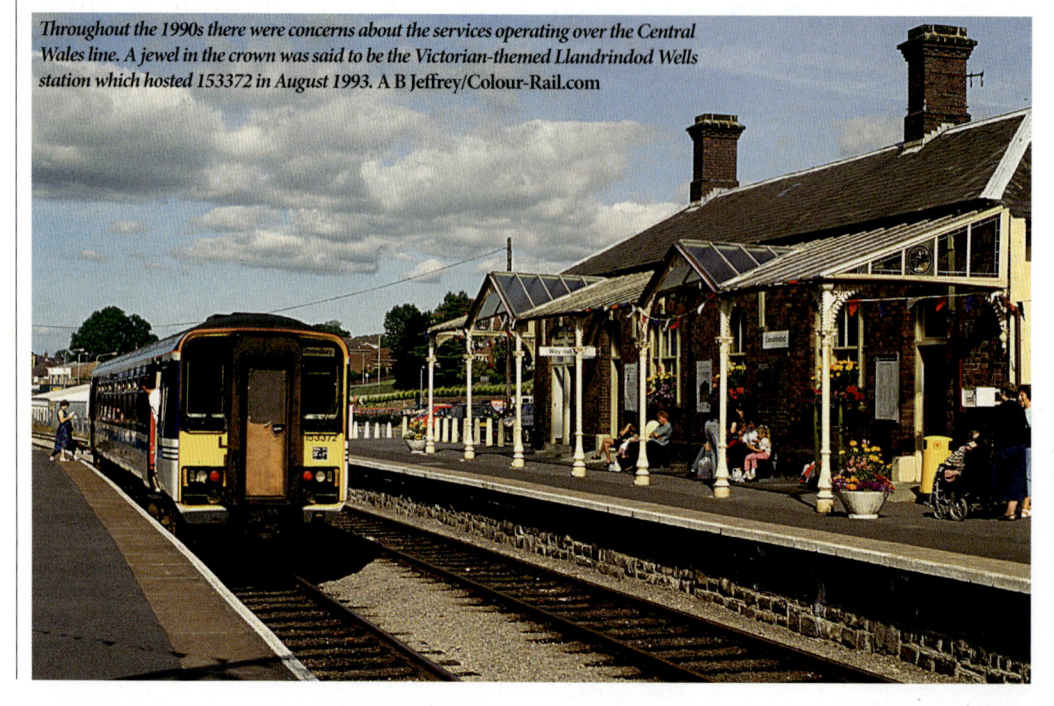

Throughout the 1990s there were concerns about the services operating over the Central Wales line. A jewel in the crown was said to be the Victorian-themed Llandrindod Wells station which hosted 153372 in August 1993. A B Jeffrey/Colour-Rail.com

10
Britain's Railways in the 1990s

1990

of the wall, local residents whose homes were invaded by the sea were planning to seek appropriate compensation from the railway.

The ageing architecture of a number of stations and increasing interest in accurate restorations led to many railway buildings being given listed structure status meaning that repair and restoration work had to be carried out in accordance with stringent regulations. An interesting project took place at Llandrindod where the county council contributed £33,000 to its 're-Victorianisation'. A new passing loop at Knighton was also to be provided to give more operational flexibility, this breaking up the current longest single line section in the country at 30 miles.

A long running rebuilding project was that of Liverpool Street station which would see the provision of a pleasant concourse area at the expense of condemning most platform space to 'life under artificial light' due to the construction of a vast concrete raft carrying various city buildings on top.

A piece of history which belonged to the previous decade was the closing of West Blyth coal staithes on December 31, 1989, these being the last timber decked staithes belonging to BR. These were to be replaced in the Autumn of 1990 by the provision of a rail connection to the NCB staithes at Bates near Blyth.

The Government of the day approved plans for part of an East-West Crossrail project with a line connecting Paddington and Liverpool Street with an estimated travel time of ten minutes. Numerous proposals were under discussion to (re) open lines for passenger use along with a number of new stations, the first of which to come into use was Meadowhall to serve the new shopping centre to the northeast of Sheffield city centre, this taking place on September 5. Woodsmore and Worle both joined the network in October. Alongside expansion proposals the business sectors were trying to balance the books and seeking to remove loss making services from the timetable which in some cases would even result in line closures, with Yorkshire being a hotbed of such moves in 1990 where the Passenger Transport Executives (PTEs) were trying to expand services but the Provincial sector was pruning them. Not resulting in a line closure however, as the route was heavily used by freight traffic, was the decision by Intercity to withdraw the Cleveland Executive HST which was the only passenger service to use the Eaglescliffe to Northallerton route. Illustrating how things change, today the line sees up to four passenger trains per hour. Another change relevant to today was the final clearing of the track at Curzon Street goods depot, in Birmingham which is now under redevelopment as the terminus for HS2 services in the city. The Cadbury World attraction at Bourneville was opened with the local station receiving large quantities of purple paint work to promote the attraction.

The loco liveries were constantly evolving at this time and a new one was added to the list, that being applied to engines allocated to the Civil Engineer's department and being overall dark grey with a yellow band approximately two thirds of the way up the bodyside. Another new livery to appear, but this time on passenger stock was that for the West Midlands Centro area being basically blue and grey with yellow and green bands with 150116 being the first unit to carry it

Stock changes

The year saw the delivery of 14 Class 60s, the final 15 each of 90s and 91s along with the arrival of the 59/1s 59101-4 with new electric units being 319161-76, some class 320s,321s and 322s plus DMUs 158702-59. Condemnation of units saw 20 electric multiple units (EMUs) go from the Southern early in the year followed by a similar number of 303s and 311s in October when the 320s

The rebuilding of Liverpool Street station was a long project and still had a couple of years to run as the new decade started. Much of the work caused inconvenience to passengers, but the task in hand seen here was well away for the normal passenger circulation areas. T Owen/Colour-Rail.com

The operational demise of Blyth coal staithes came in 1990. Enthusiasts of a certain age might well remember their reasonably close encounter with them while taking the ferry from South to North Blyth during shed bashing activities in the 1960s, this picture dating from July 28 1966 taken during one such crossing of the river. A B Jeffrey/Colour-Rail.com

A small number of new stations opened in 1990 with Meadowhall near Sheffield being the first. It is seen here shortly after completion. P Hughes/Colour-Rail.com

entered service, with some 90 first generation DMU cars condemned towards the year end, in theory balancing the number of Cl 158 units available for work although many of the condemned units appeared to have been out of use for some time. Also out were prototype units 140001 and 151003/4. The first new EMU of the year arrived for Southern in December this being 456001.

As for the existing locomotive fleet, there were a small number of loco withdrawals in January, almost balanced by re-instatements involving classes 20, 31, 33, 47 and 85. One engine entered departmental stock that being 08600 which became 97800. However no less than 40 engines were noted as having been named in the last in the last few weeks, these almost exclusively being on the books of Tinsley shed.

Each month onwards the occasional new loco was delivered with a small number of withdrawals, usual around eight to ten along with two or three re-instatements to traffic. However, in October no fewer than 17 Class 20s we condemned - in addition to four that had gone in September - despite the fact that the delayed introduction of the Class 60s was supposed to see Class 20s retained to cover their duties. The month also saw a major re-allocation of locos.

Early rolling stock deliveries comprised just driving van trailers (DVTs) for use on West Coast duties.

An interesting loco re-instated to capital stock on November 23 was Class 25 25912. Originally 25322 it became well known when named as *Tamworth Castle* being frequently displayed at open days. It became 25912 in 1984 and moved to departmental duties in 1987, officially numbered ADB968027 although that was not carried.

59101 went to Derby from Newport via Whatley for acceptance tests and 59104 ran trials at up to 80mph between Derby and Cricklewood hauling a test coach and five sleeper carriages.

The motive power situation as the decade opened was that no new locomotives were notified as entering traffic in January.

The once stable Southern EMU numbering system had, since the arrival of TOPS and a series of refurbishments and upgrades, become a challenge for the most ardent number takers with numerous changes such as the renumbering of Class 421/4 units from 1814 to 1825 becoming 1301-12 to be joined by new conversions 1313-1316 from previously numbered 1252/44/64/41 with the first two originally allocated the numbers 1826/7.

Although some of the HST fleet had been in service for some 15 years the fleet did see constant planned changes of formation as well as maintenance swaps. Moves planned for the start of the summer timetable saw some sets already having seven carriages receiving an additional vehicle. 'Surplus' carriages were also being converted from First to Second Class use and renumbered accordingly but not in any specific order. Of note was the official storage of power cars 43167/70 in May, these being two

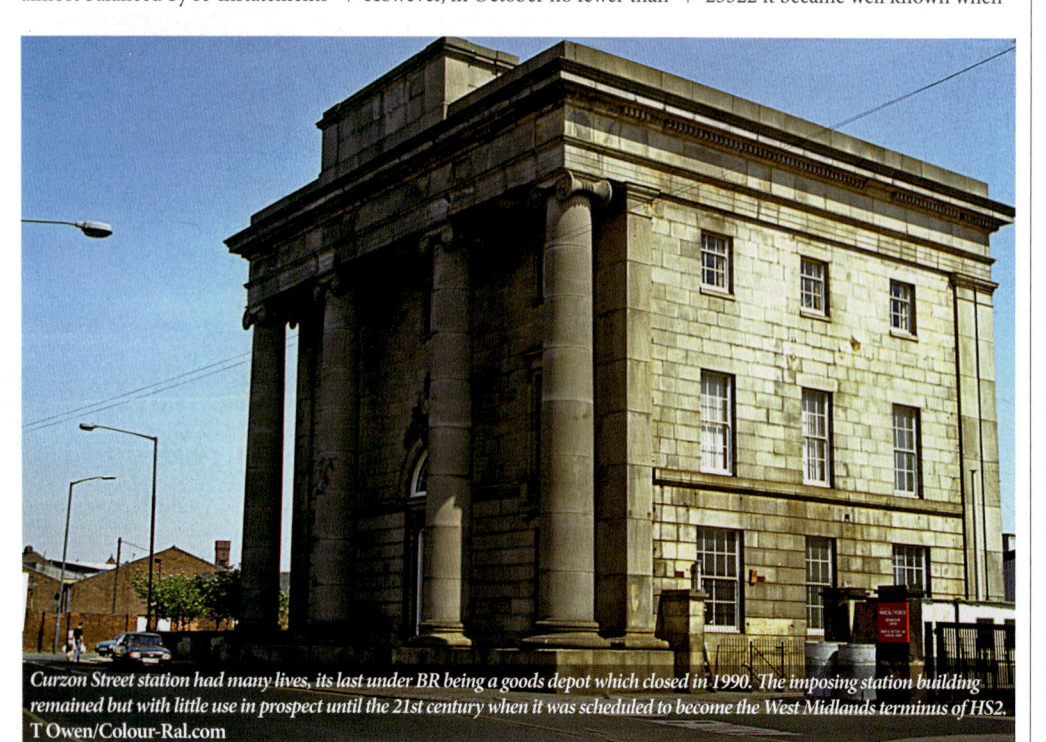

Curzon Street station had many lives, its last under BR being a goods depot which closed in 1990. The imposing station building remained but with little use in prospect until the 21st century when it was scheduled to become the West Midlands terminus of HS2. T Owen/Colour-Ral.com

Britain's Railways in the 1990s

1990

of the four fitted with Mirrlees engines. 43167 made a fairly rapid but temporary return to service.

An advantage of the Nationalised railway was that there was regular and structured reporting about locomotives and rolling stock whereas 'private' businesses tended to treat such information as commercially sensitive and consciously prevented publication. So, the BR annual freight stock inventory was still available in 1990 and showed that the total stock stood at 20,887 vehicles -approximately 500 fewer than one year earlier. However, the total would not have included any leased stock of which Tiphook were the main provider and it sold 181 POA wagons for carrying steel scrap to BR in March.

The Network South East brand was going from strength to strength but away from the Southern region many of its services were operated by first-generation DMUs. With growing passenger numbers permission was given to order some replacement stock and despite the fact that the class 158s were only just entering traffic a new design dubbed the Networker had been developed for some Southern region electric stock and similar carriages in the shape of the Class 165 were ordered for use on commuter services from Paddington and Marylebone. In late 1990 a further order for what were at the time described as Class 165/2 units was placed, these being fitted with air conditioning for express duties. The order for Class 158 units was also modified with the final 66 carriages being 'cancelled' and replaced by one for 69 carriages as Class 159 for duties from Waterloo to Exeter with delivery scheduled for 1993. These units would include First Class accommodation, unlike most of the 158s as built, and would have a different engine type.

A new livery was unleashed on the system, this being the Parcels Sector red and black colour scheme with 47474 being the first recipient.

In the course of delivery was the stock for the East Coast route, particularly the Driving Van Trailers (DVT). As a stop gap for the late delivery of the DVTs the Eastern Region had been employing specially modified HST driving cars on duties from Kings Cross and they were still so employed at the start of 1990 but they would revert to conventional use in due course although always identifiable as they had been fitted with buffers.

A new but small class of EMUs, the 322s, entered service on August 9. These units were intended for Stanstead Express duties but the new service was not scheduled to start until March 1991

It was intended that the Scottish region would be the first recipients of the Class 158 units but their non-arrival saw contingency plans being developed including the retention of locomotives and stock that should have moved elsewhere. Edinburgh and Glasgow to Inverness services were to be turned over to operation by push pull sets and all of that fleet were to be based at Inverness as space was required at Craigentinny for East Coast electrification works. Glasgow-Aberdeen services were to be worked by Class 156 units coming from East Anglia whilst loco and stock formations would replace 156s from Aberdeen to Inverness. A consequence of 156s on the Aberdeen to Glasgow route would be no First Class accommodation and a maximum speed of 75mph rather than the planned 100mph capability. Scotrail was in 'growth mode' with some ten new stations planned for early opening. Another consequence of the use of Class 156 units when replacing three-car first-generation sets was the reduction in seating capacity leading to serious overcrowding on some routes. The first appearance of a 158 on test in Scotland was January 10 at Edinburgh and it reached Inverness the next day. Further plans for 158s were for use on trans-Pennine duties, East Anglia to the Northwest and on long distance Western region trains where it emerged that the intention was that they would replace the still very new Class 155s and that those units would be converted to single car units and reclassed as 153. The first use of Class 158s on passenger duties were recorded as September 17 when four were on Edinburgh-Glasgow duties. Just a few days earlier Scotrail had also put its Class 320 units into service on the North electric routes in Glasgow.

Hunslet Transportation Projects was awarded a contract to construct 37 EMUs (class 323) for use on the Birmingham Cross City line and on some routes from Manchester.

Attempts to modernise the railway were always fraught with problems, sometimes of the railway's own making. Driver-only operation (DOO) was one such instance from Euston to Northampton and beyond where, when the new stock for the service was delivered it was claimed by the unions that all of the required station mirrors were incorrectly located relative to their cab seating position as apparently the Class 321s had the driver's seat some 18 inches further towards the centre of the driving cab than the

The year saw the arrival of 59101-4 from across the pond for use by Yeoman on aggregates traffic. All arrived at Newport docks and with the bogies apparently chocked in the required position the body of 59104 is swung over the side of the ship on October 20. Colour-Rail.com

Members of classes 319 through to 322 arrived during the year. Seen in Southern region territory was 319163 at Streatham Hill depot on October 21. The units would see service on Thameslink duties. D Pye/Colour-Rail.com

Britain's Railways in the 1990s

158701 had the distinction of being the only class member to arrive in the 1980s. As the class leader it spent many months on tests and trials and although nominally a Scottish region asset it is seen here at Swindon on March 30. A B Jeffrey/Colour-Rail

To the traveller HST cars 43167-70 looked just like any other HST but the four were fitted with a Mirrlees engine and like most non-standard pieces of equipment spent periods out of service awaiting parts. 43167 was the worst afflicted and indeed 43168 seen here enjoyed a more active life in 1990 and was photographed at Plymouth en route from Penzance to Edinburgh on August 30. John E Henderson/Colour-Rail.com

stock that was in use previously and which had been used to set the mirror positions. Correcting this caused the postponement of DOO by several months.

Services

With increasing passenger demand, service improvements were being announced although it was a 'drip feed' process. One such was the increase in the frequency of services between Leeds and Manchester to three per hour comprising Hull-Manchester, Scarborough-Manchester and Newcastle-Liverpool. Many were loco hauled at the time with an expectation that Class 158s would replace these but not until 1991.

Proposals were put forward to return Maesteg to the passenger network and the government approved the finance for an investigation into the scheme to go ahead. New or re-opened stations were suggested at

1990

Tondu, Aberkenfig, Sarn, Pencoed and Pontyclun.

The start of the year saw an investigation into the running of through trains from Swindon to Peterborough, this requiring the re-instatement of the line from Bicester to Bletchley. The current East West Rail project does not target Peterborough, but it will at least allow travellers to get as far as Bletchley when it is completed.

An example of the changes seen in the last thirty or so years was the service only provided with County Council support from Worcester via Bromsgrove as far as Barnt Green where it connected with Cross City trains that provided a still fairly sparse service on the Birmingham-Redditch line, although electrification of that route had just been approved. The Bromsgrove service was provided by a single car DMU on a two hourly frequency. Today Bromsgrove is severed by an often over crowded hourly service from Hereford to Birmingham with an additional two trains per hour on the Cross City route. Another location under threat was Pershore that enjoyed just one through train to and from Paddington each day with an occasional DMU stopper working from Oxford to Hereford. Today it has an hourly service to and from the capital.

Operations

Traditionally EMUs worked throughout their lives on one route but with the growth in electrification surplus units did on occasions wander from their traditional home turf an example of which was the move of some Class 307 units from East Anglia to Neville Hill this happening as the final batch of Class 321s arrived for duties from Liverpool Street. A special train was operated on June 30 to mark the removal of all the 307s from service in East Anglia.

A very quick outline of motive power in 1990 was that in East Anglia Class 86 electrics powered the London-Norwich services with most other services in East Anglia being worked by units with classes 156 and 321 being the latest arrivals. East Coast services were in the hands of HSTs with Class 91s just starting duties to Leeds. Suburban services in the London area were in the process of being switched from class 317 to 321 with the former moving to the Midland mainline where again HSTs held sway on longer journeys. The West Coast route was in the process of converting from loco hauled sets to push pull operation. Suburban duties from Marylebone and Paddington were in the hands of first-generation DMUs with HSTs doing all the main line work from the latter supplemented by class 47s on stock for peak hour outer suburban trains. Services from Southern London termini were almost all EMU worked with Class 455 being the most recent units delivered. The major exception was the services to Exeter which in theory at least were Class 50 worked although class 33 and 47 substitutes were frequent. Elsewhere around the country, with the exception of a number of cross country duties powered by HSTs DMUs held sway being a mixture of first- and second- generation types except on routes such as Edinburgh- Glasgow, The Highland lines, Newcastle-Liverpool, Cardiff-Crewe and a small number of other intermediate length journeys.

One notable cessation of loco worked services took place when through trains from Liverpool Street to Kings Lynn ceased on May 12. These had been worked

Sector livery took many forms and in 1990 Parcels sector set out to make their locos easily identifiable by painting them red and black. 47474 was the first recipient of the new colours but appears to be working anything but a parcels at Oxford on May 26. D Pye/Colour-Rail.com

The Class 322 EMUs were sourced specifically to work Stanstead Express duties and the class leader 322481 was displayed at Crewe Works ahead of its launch into service. Ultimately they became wanderers around the system. Colour-Rail.com

by Class 47s allocated to Stratford and left the once famous depot with no diagrammed loco hauled passenger duties. Another long standing loco hauled service to end was 'The Cobbler', an unofficial title bestowed on the once per day fast service from Northampton to Euston and return.

With the East Coast electrification programme nearing completion, which would result in a number of HST sets becoming available for use elsewhere, a demonstration train ran from Birmingham to Weymouth on November 17, this bringing an HST to Bournemouth for the first time.

The coming of the 90 mph freight train appeared to be on the cards with the announcement of the hiring of twenty five SNCF 'Multifret' wagons to operate a Harwich to Manchester and Glasgow service conveying 'swap bodies' with 90mph running authorised throughout from Willesden to Glasgow. The service was to start in February.

BRUTES, the blue high-sided trollies used to transfer mail and parcels on platforms had been around for probably 30 years but an incident with one becoming stuck on a line crossing and nearly hit by a train prompted at least all of those used on the Western Region to be placed under severe use restrictions and requiring permission from the signalman before any line crossing was attempted, seeing the temporary return of much older trollies and barrows which apparently had been retained 'just in case'. Ultimately with the cessation of both parcels traffic and mail by rail, trollies of any type would become redundant allowing the railways to present the soulless platforms of today. That said, in 1990 the industry was still interested in carrying parcels and found an additional job for BRUTES to carry parcels for Track 29, a service said to fill the gap between Red Star parcels and standard distribution services. The BRUTES used on the service were to be fitted with hoods and would be loaded into dedicated trains running at up to 90mph with guaranteed delivery by 17.00 the next day.

The new Class 60 locos began to be recorded with 60004/8 being noted at Thornaby in early February although only for crew training duties. Some 35 were due in service by the end of June but the usual teething problems, particularly concerning the

The Class 50s were nominally in charge of all Waterloo-Exeter services but as their numbers and reliability decreased there were frequent substitutions. However 50003 seemed to be alive and well on September 1 as it 'hoovered' into Templecombe with a complete turnout of NSE livery. R Siviter/Colour-Rail.com

1990

Entry into traffic of the new Class 60s was very slow and they were banned from operational duties for much of the year and indeed like 60002 seen here with an 822XX DVT, spent much time under test. D Stocker/Colour-Rail.com

suspension and slow speed control saw only 60001 formally accepted into traffic by that time. However the optimism was short-lived with an edict issued by BR in early July that members of the class must not be used on revenue earning duties until further notice with a range of issues to be resolved by Brush. As a consequence a number of Class 20s and 47s were to receive life extensions modifications and overhauls. Three members of the class finally entered revenue earning service from Thornaby on November 5. Classes 56 and 58 found reasonably regular use on passenger turns when the power was off on the West Coast line and complete trains were 'dragged' through the affected area. However, use on a scheduled passenger duty elsewhere was indeed rare but 56035 worked from Salisbury to Waterloo and back on March 16 following the failure of the booked Class 50.

Instead of reports of snow and ice leading to disruption in January and February, high winds and flooding were causing delays and cancellations with overhead electrification lines suffering particularly. This was a new problem for East Coast commuters who until recently had enjoyed the relative security of rattling DMUs to carry them to and from work. A washout on the Gloucester-Lydney route saw buses substituted but in less than seven days a temporary station was constructed at Over to reduce the 'bustitution' section to just two miles, this remaining in use for around three weeks. The whole country was affected by the storms with for instance no trains running in Cornwall on January 25. Another of the line blockages caused Paddington-Plymouth HSTs and some cross country services to be diverted to the ex-Southern route via Honiton. However due to much of it being single track only a small number of through services could be provided. The Southern region itself saw severe disruption in the January storm with some luckless passengers who left Waterloo at 10.30 ending up being transferred to a bus near Winchester at midnight.

As a result of storms on Jan 25, Bristol Temple Meads station was closed for a time. A special HST was then provided to run to Birmingham later being extended to Newcastle. Passengers for the northwest were required to change at Birmingham New Street where an EMU, probably a Class 310 was provide to Crewe. However this then went forward to Carlisle where it was possibly the first (and last?) of its type to be seen there. One of the new Class 91s, 91011, appeared at Euston on March 2 when, while out on test at Bletchley, was used to rescue a Liverpool-Euston service which it then worked to the capital. Another 'one off' thought to be caused by diagram disruption due to the weather saw the use of a Western region based HST set on the Flying Scotsman on February 27. Flood damage in 1989 had seen the bridge across the River Ness at Inverness washed away and ever since the Far North lines had been worked in isolation with a road link to the rest of Scotland. Replacement spans were craned into place on 11 February, just one year and four days after the bridge collapse. The line was re-opened at the start of the summer timetable in May.

Come August and it was the 'excessively hot' weather, which was causing problems with delays due to track faults, sagging wires and lineside fires. One individual decided that the weather was good enough for him to sunbathe between the tracks at Ravensthorpe with delays to trains until he was forcibly removed. Apparently, it was also a very dry summer which led to a ban on carriage washing using mains water at Ashford and Ramsgate. An independent water source was identified resulting in the daily running of a train composed of two 45 tonne tanks powered by a Motor Luggage van to collect the water and take it to the two depots.

The winter of 1990/1 appeared as though it was going to be more 'traditional' with six inches of snow disrupting services in the north on December 8.

Occasionally a humorous incident (depending on your point ➤

17

71000 Duke of Gloucester made its debut runs in preservation in 1990 and is seen here heading towards Birmingham near Tamworth. P Chancellor/Colour-Rail.com

of view) occurred, such as when a night reballasting operation was planned. With Permanent Way (PW) staff brought in specially on night shift to carry out the work the ballast train duly arrived, only for the team to discover that all of the wagons were empty. Following a very relaxed night 'shift' the crew returned 24 hours later - fortunately the error was not repeated.

A sign of things to come was the introduction of a ban on smoking on a number of NSE suburban services south of the Thames.

Much like current times trains were being deleted from timetables due to a lack of staff, this being particularly noted on Southern commuter lines and despite the formal cancellations travellers continued to encounter frequent problems on a daily basis these being exacerbated by stock shortages as well.

Railway open days and exhibitions were a feature of the time, one such being at Gloucester on July 1. Around 20 mainline engines were on show including 90010 along with a number of heritage diesels. Excursions to the event were run along with trains running to/from Birmingham and Bristol worked by a range of motive power including 56034 and 58004. A similar event at Cambridge saw special trains formed of Class 310 EMUs being loco hauled with 37218, 56065 and 73103/29 noted.

Heritage

The decade opened with a relatively small pool of operational main line engines which included 5080, 6998, 777, 34027, 5407, 45596, 2005, 3442, and 80080 but a number of 'big names' were almost ready for a mainline debut.

The year was to see the entry into service of a number of high profile mainline performers. King 6024 was the initial of these to undergo mainline trials when it ran to Derby making it the first appearance of the type on the line from Birmingham. Out on test in February was A4 60009 *Union of South Africa* although temporarily named *Osprey* due to political unrest in South Africa. Next to undergo its test run saw the much anticipated return to action of 71000 *Duke of Gloucester* making a first mainline appearance since 1962. Also eagerly awaited was the return of 46229 *Duchess of Hamilton* which was tested at the end of March. With 35028 *Clan Line* also available, class eight motive power from each BR constituent plus the BR Standard design could appear on the mainline for the first time in the heritage era. More super power in the shape

Due to political unrest in South Africa A4 60009 underwent a name and number change for a few months becoming 60027 and carrying the name Merlin. It is seen here departing from Crewe. P Chancellor/Colour-Rail

18   *Britain's Railways in the 1990s*

1990

of 4472 *Flying Scotsman,* recently returned from a visit to Australia, and 46203 *Princess Margaret Rose* also joined the mainline fleet by the end of May. However most found themselves without employment in August when BR imposed a ban on steam engines due to the perceived high fire risk. At the same time the provisional programme for mainline steam up to May 1991 envisaged a train almost every week from December to May on one of Marylebone-Stratford, Skipton-Carlisle or the North Wales coast routes.

A constant in the heritage story since the late 1960s was the saving of locomotives from the Barry Dock sidings used by Dai Woodham. However by mid-1990 all of those lines had been removed and any cutting up work, mainly of wagons, was to be carried out on two short sidings adjacent to the old Railway Works.

Heritage lines undertaking track laying included the Gloucestershire Warwickshire, westwards from Winchcombe, B'oness & Kinneil from Birkhill to Manuel and the Llangollen which was approaching Deeside Halt while Peak Rail was in the process of moving stock from its Buxton base to Darley Dale.

Deeside saw the first train for 25 years when Manor 7828 arrived there with ECS on January 6.

King 6023 which had been resident for restoration at Bristol Temple Meads since its rescue from Dai Woodham's Barry scrapyard was loaded in bits onto a number of wagons on March 5 for removal to Didcot and delivery to the Great Western Society there.

A growing trend in the preservation movement was for the major railways to carry out contract restoration work for other lines or engine owners and the Midland Railway Centre had work in hand on boilers from 42765, and 92214 with that from an 8F possibly arriving from Peak Rail. Another growth area was the rescue of redundant modern traction classes with for instance Peak 45133 moving to the Peak Rail site at Buxton.

New preservation schemes were still being proposed, one such was the Somerset & Avon Railway which wished to reopen the GWR line from Frome to Radstock, one of many that did not succeed. The other side of the coin was TWERPS, a group proposing to re-instate trains from Tunbridge Wells to Eridge with the society already occupying the station site at Eridge. Another fledgling group was the Coventry Steam Railway Centre based at Baginton Airport, this having stock but no running line. Although evolving in later years to concentrate particularly on EMUs it was forced to disband when the site was required for redevelopment.

The Swanage Railway appeared likely to be allowed to run trains into the bay platform at Wareham and hired three carriages from a former Hastings line unit to run the service. Track laying reached a milestone in mid-year with laying operations reaching Corfe Castle station. Another line where track laying was making progress was on the Isle of Wight with Ashey being reached from Haven Street.

The Kent & East Sussex Railway opened an extension to Bodiam on May 19 and the Llangollen Railway duly opened through to Deeside in April. The Great Central Railway announced plans to open through to Leicester and create a double track section of the line by 1995.

A new entrant to the heritage scene - the Bure Valley Railway, at 15 in gauge and running from Aylesham to Wroxham - opened on July 10 while a two-foot gauge line on the former track bed of the Leadhills & Wanlockhead line was under construction. Construction of a station at Leadhills was under way in July and some stock was on site.

Barrow Hill shed was scheduled for imminent closure in late 1990 and the Engine Shed Society approached English Heritage to try and get the building listed as a site of historic interest.

The Great Central Railway grew almost to its current length on November 18 when the extension from Rothley to Birstall platform, just short of the proposed Leicester North station was opened. With no run round loop trains had to be propelled on the return if steam worked although the intention was to use a DMU on most services. New in traffic at the railway was Merchant Navy 35005 *Canadian Pacific.*

Not everything in the preservation world was 'sweetness and light' as a move by the Ffestiniog Railway to purchase the 22-mile track bed of the Welsh Highland line was contested by the WHR 1964 group which was operating over a ¾ mile section of the route neat Porthmadoc.

The Severn Valley Railway opened a new boiler repair shop on October 29 running a 'royal train' to convey HRH the Duke of Gloucester from Kidderminster to Bridgnorth for the official opening ceremony.

The autumn saw the arrival of three steam locomotives from Finland. All were five-foot gauge and had to stand on suitable track panels at a site near Sudbury. One was Tr class 2-8-2 1077 which in recent months has made headlines in the heritage railway press by being 'rediscovered' under masses of brambles, having apparently not moved from its initial UK home. ∎

During the year a number of steam engines were imported from Finland through Felixstowe docks. It was hoped that they would find use in the UK but as they needed to be regauged it seems the plans came to naught and 1077 seen here resided in undergrowth until 'rediscovered' in 2022. Colour-Rail.com

Britain's Railways in the 1990s

19

The demise of Speedlink was announced during the year removing many freight services from the network overnight. 47016 was noted at Cardiff on one such train in August 1989. D Pye/Colour-Rail.com

1991

FAREWELL TO THE REGIONS

As part of its transformation leading to privatisation BR proposed to disband regional structures with the Southern being the first to succumb, this being scheduled to happen in April. In some ways this appeared to be a strange choice as of all the regions it was the most self-contained simply because of the use of third rail electrification. On the Western a re-organisation in the southwest saw the abolition of area managers who were replaced by operating and station managers. Five of the former looked after all of the lines in Somerset, Devon and Cornwall but Intercity had responsibility for the mainline from Plymouth to Swindon, Regional Railways for all other passenger lines in Devon and the whole of Cornwall, except Salisbury to Exmouth Junction (NSE) and Railfreight which looked after all of the 'freight only' lines. All as clear as mud really!

The Scottish region ceased to exist from May 27 when Scotrail became the first single geographic profit centre, although it remained part of the Regional Railways empire. Intercity services south from Edinburgh and Glasgow plus all freight were not included in the Scotrail organisation. No doubt it kept many accountants busy as even individual platforms were designated as Scotrail or Intercity.

A new livery for Regional Railways was announced with a grey base colour with grey, blue in two shades and white being used in bands. Merseyrail launched a new livery variation employing yellow, black and white.

Property developers were eyeing up Birmingham New Street station for redevelopment 'along the lines of changes made at Liverpool Street' while Centro claimed that the station was inadequate for its needs and was looking at opening a replacement at Saltley.

The first 'passenger train' traversed the Channel Tunnel on February 12 when a number of 'manriders', normally used to convey tunnel workers, brought around 100 invited guests arriving in Dover from France. The railway press of the time made frequent mention of planned terminals around the country that were to be used specifically for handling freight arriving via the tunnel with nine sites identified. Plans for the passenger service were revealed with hourly trains from Waterloo to both Paris and Brussels with Amsterdam and Frankfurt suggested as later destinations. Starting points within the UK were given as Manchester, Edinburgh, Glasgow, Swansea and Plymouth. A proposal to spend £140m on a new station to be known as Ashford International was rejected by the Government who only wished to spend some £8m which it was said would only provide basic facilities at a site one mile away from the BR station. Proposals for the high

Britain's Railways in the 1990s

1991

as the station had seen a 25% increase in passengers in the last five years but this would sow the seeds for a major rail disaster to occur there in 1999.

A story that was to have a long life was the proposal to convert the track bed of the line from Luton to Dunstable into a busway, this not becoming a reality until 2013. Following on from the 1990 suggestion of a high speed link between Paddington and Liverpool Street a much larger 'Crossrail' proposal was made, this being for a joint venture between BR and LT for trains to run from Reading to East London to link with the Docklands system with the possibility of running through to Southend eight and twelve car formations were envisaged with up to twelve trains per hour. No target opening date was mentioned.

The long running rebuilding of Liverpool Street station was finally deemed complete with an official opening ceremony being performed on December 5.

An electrification scheme that was completed in mid-March was that from Carstairs to Edinburgh Waverley, this being ahead of that from Kings Cross to Edinburgh where wiring in the Newcastle area had yet to be finished. Class 91s had been active on crew training for a period but in early April the class began trial running through to Carstairs. The East Coast route became operational from June 10 with three trains in each direction being worked by a Class 91 with Mk IV stock with additional duties being added for each of the first few weeks. A consequence of the completion of work on the East Coast mainline was the closure of the Pelaw valley line, which though nominally a freight route, was used extensively for diversions for passenger services during the installation period.

The success of a new station at Yate, between Gloucester and Bristol caused embarrassment as it was only built to handle two-car trains which led to frequent overcrowding. Proposals were soon put forward for an extension to allow four-car units to be used.

The Docklands Light Railway which had opened in 1987 expanded in the 1990s and also recieved quantities of new rolling stock. 1991 saw the opening on July 29 of a line to Bank which included a tunnel section for which use by the original stock was deemed unacceptable. The first use of new B90 stock was noted on July 3. The new station at Canary Wharf was recorded as being nearly complete at that time and work was well under way for the next extension to Beckton.

It was announced that all Speedlink services would cease as July 8. Tiger Rail were proposing to run a replacement service on three routes but on alternate days as opposed to the current offering on those lines of twice per day. At the other end of the movement scale Felixstowe Docks were sold to a company based in Hong Kong who immediately announced that they intended to expand the port, much to the delight of Railfreight Distribution.

The go ahead was given for the construction of an express rail link from Paddington to Heathrow Airport which was expected to open in 1995 serving two stations within the complex with BR only sharing 20% of the costs the total being estimated at £235m.

A raft of former stations in Gloucestershire were proposed for re-opening with that at Ashchurch being heavily promoted

speed link were still to be finalised but a new station at Stratford appeared to be on the cards.

In reality the future for freight lay more in places to handle incoming container traffic rather than 'company' trains via the tunnel and PowerGen, who owned the former power station site at Hams Hall announced plans to build an International terminal there. Developments at Bristol were proposed with the building of a freight terminal at Avonmouth along with the reopening of Portbury docks which were to be dredged to allow use by larger vessels. Rail access was to be via the mothballed Portishead branch.

A remodelling of the track layout and signalling at Paddington was to be undertaken in 1992

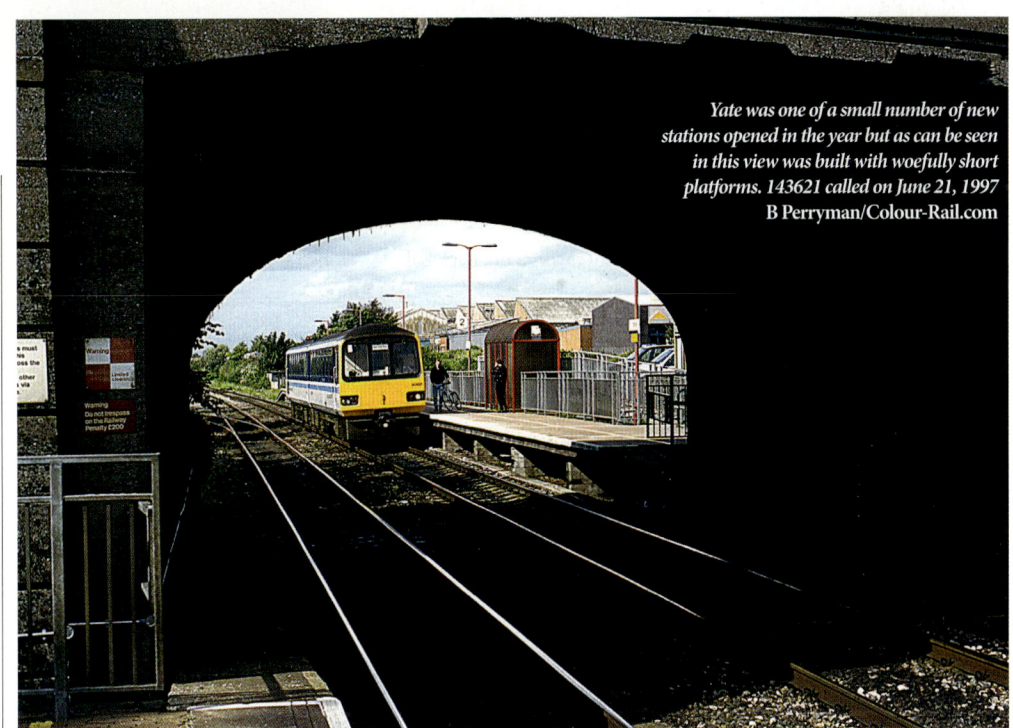

Yate was one of a small number of new stations opened in the year but as can be seen in this view was built with woefully short platforms. 143621 called on June 21, 1997
B Perryman/Colour-Rail.com

Britain's Railways in the 1990s

The year saw the completion of the rebuilding of Liverpool Street station. The circulating area was light and open but most of the platforms were covered by a concrete raft producing perpetually darkness. P Chancellor/Colour-Rail

by the Parish Council. Improved services on the Cotswold line were also up for discussion with BR suggesting that Worcester might have up to eight through trains per day to Paddington by 1993.

Stock changes

The pace of new deliveries slackend in 1991. The delivery of the final Class 91 91031 completed the East Coast fleet. Class 60s were released to traffic sporadically so while 60087 was put to stock in December some of the earlier built machines were still stored at Brush Loughborough. The highest numbered 158 was 158831 with the new Turbo 165s appearing with 20 of the two-car sets delivered for Chiltern duties. Electric multiple unit (EMU) Class 319s and 456s completed the new stock.

Loco withdrawals continued at a low level with just a handful of 08s, 31s and 47s being the main casualties. That said the railways were about to undergo perhaps the largest change in the use of motive power since the 1960s with the completion of the East Coast route electrification which would release a number of high-speed train (HST) sets, primarily for Cross Country duties.

Also finally going into service were the Class 158s. They eventually totalled around 170 units, leading to a vast 'cascade' programme releasing 156s and so on down the chain, plus replacing many of the loco-hauled sets that had provided a stopgap for a number of years. Additionally, the freight business was about to receive the Class 60s which were planned to replace up to 220 first-generation diesels.

Other orders, such as those for classes 159 and 165, would replace ageing stock but there was no major cascade programme planned in those cases. The yet to arrive 92s were intended for use solely on Channel Tunnel duties. The first Class 165 was handed over at York on February 15 and entry into service from Marylebone started on September 9.

The year started with well in excess of 300 first-generation diesel multiple unit (DMU) sets at work, mostly in two and three car formations with many of the cars approaching at least 35 years in service.

BR published their annual stock return, this always covering the financial year which ended on March 31, 1991. It showed that 56 engines were taken into stock of classes 60, 90 and 91 and 127 were withdrawn with Class 20 having the highest number of casualties. No fewer than 56 engines were renumbered. The major first-generation classes remaining were 08 (422), 31 (174), 37 (304), and 47 (422). A totally unexpected withdrawal in late September was that of 56042, the loco only being thirteen years old. It appeared to have spent much of the time since receiving fire damage in 1983 out of service.

The creep of 'improved' safety measures was being felt with an edict from the Railway Inspectorate that all platforms must be sufficiently long and high to allow access from all doors of a train. Of course, since the start

All of the Class 91s were in service by mid-year and were in charge, along with HSTs, of all East Coast services. 91003 plus others are viewed at Kings Cross on October 24. D Pye/Colour-Rail.com

1991

of the railways, trains had not always fitted on to the platform but strangely passengers seemed to be able to work around this by the use of common sense! It was estimated that implementation might cost £50m and lead to shorter trains being provided on some routes. The authorities were demanding compliance by October. Another requirement was that all platforms must be lit at night. This caused great concern on the Central Wales line where many were not so provided but as it operated under a Light Railway Order it was deemed exempt from such requirements.

Scotrail planned to work the Edinburgh-North Berwick service with EMUs and a Class 307 had moved north for crew training. However local opposition and the apparent unreliability of the units in use in West Yorkshire led to a change of plan with redundant Class 305 units now becoming the chosen traction with the first arriving in late February for training duties.

With mobile phones not yet being in anything like widespread use, many HST sets had carriages being fitted with conventional pay phones.

The first Class 153 unit, converted from a 155, 57304 forming 153304 was noted on test on June 26. Heaton and Cardiff were the first depots to receive the type. An order was announced for the air conditioned version of Class 165, this being for 21 units forming Class 166. The year started with an announcement of the approval of a scheme to return trams to Sheffield at a cost of £230m and was said in the press release to be 'more ambitious' than that already approved for Manchester. The first trams were expected to run in 1993 with completion of the scheme in 1995.

Work on the Manchester Metrolink route to Bury required the existing BR line to be closed which resulted in the wholesale withdrawal of the Class 504 units that worked the service and bringing to an end the use of the unique 1200v 3rd rail system in the UK. In order for work to begin on the line to Altrincham, the BR service ceased on December 24 while the first trams for the Bury line started trials in November. The Tyne Wear Metro reached its furthest point north when a new section was opened from Kenton Bank Foot to Newcastle Airport on November 17. Construction of Channel Tunnel stock commenced. The body shells were built on the continent and shipped to MCW Birmingham for fitting out. The EMU sets were to be known as Class 373.

Services

Despite the demise of Speedlink services the carriage of parcels and mail continued to be an attractive business and Rail Express Systems was launched to handle all the Royal Mail traffic plus Red Star and Track 29 parcels. This included a revised livery for the Class 47 and 90s employed with the original red and black scheme being enlivened by the use of less black although a panel extended down the bodyside with four light blue blocks superimposed.

The branch line to Stanstead Airport officially opened on January 29 with various dignitaries present and arriving on 322481/3 from Liverpool Street. It had been hoped that trains would start running from Wakefield to Pontefract but this was postponed until 1992 due to an apparent shortage of funds- although it was agreed that new stations would be built at Pontefract Tanshelf, Featherstone and Streethouse. Proposals costing an estimated £15m were put forward to provide an hourly service from Salisbury to Exeter which would involve both signalling and track alterations. Depending on the approval for expenditure these were projected to be completed any time between 1993 and 2006.

New units arriving on the Southern saw the demise of the once ubiquitous 4EPB units with the exception of 5001, this being retained and repainted green for occasional use and display at open days. Another restoration project was that of 303048 on the Scottish region, this appearing in its original mock Caledonian blue colour scheme. Pre grouping rolling stock, being at best approaching seventy years of age, would not be expected to survive on a modern railway but six vehicles remained on the books in departmental stock, although four were condemned. The winner and still active was built by the LNWR in 1907 and was converted for use as an electrification coach carrying number LDM395328.

For reasons now lost in the mists of time the 1991 Summer timetable was not implemented until the start of July although some lines did see major changes in early June. The schedule changes saw another outbreak of loco re-allocations no doubt also related to the many changes occurring with the widespread introduction of both classes 60 and 158.

A new electrification plan emerged, that being to extend the Mersey third rail system from Hooton to Chester with a projected go live date of the end of 1993. The standard 25Kv system however was to be used for the Wharfdale and Airdale scheme taking the wires to Skipton with a planned opening in 1994. A completely new line was envisaged on the other side of the Pennines to provide a rail link from Manchester Piccadilly to the airport with an envisaged four trains per hour.

Operations

Mail and parcels traffic was still a major source of income for

The entry into service of the Class 60s was a very protracted affair with a number stored at the Brush works in Loughborough pending modification and approval. 60026 was among the residents in September 1990.
T Owen/Colour-Rail.com

the railways in the early 1990s with for instance an observer at Reading on January 16 reporting that parcels van trains occupied no fewer than five platforms shortly before midnight.

Despite the arrival of the Class 158s a number of services appeared to be desperately short of serviceable locos and or stock. Frequently mentioned were Salisbury-Exeter trains and also services operated by DMUs based at Reading. However even the more modern provisions such as the Liverpool Street-Norwich line and West Coast trains from Euston were affected, the latter apparently because of faults with the DVTs . This led to problems because the timetable was set up for a quick turnaround of trains at Euston but when DVTs were not provided locos had to be shunt released before being able to return north.

The railways had for many years been the subject of industrial unrest, but the start of the decade saw only occasional and localised action often lasting just one day. More disruptive at the time were security alerts. In 1990 they occurred at a low level, but on February 18, 1991 IRA bombs exploded at Paddington and Victoria stations, the latter killing one person and injuring 43. All of the London termini were immediately closed causing massive disruption with passengers stranded on trains that were on final approach and all others were detrained at suburban stations to make their own way into the capital. Most stations reopened late in the day but subsequently many false alarms continued to cause problems for several days. A consequence of the attacks was that many stations had their rubbish bins and lockers removed. Security alerts continued throughout the year and there was another explosion, this time at Latchmere Junction, on December 16.

The end appeared in sight for the Folkestone Harbour branch with the announcement by Sealink that the ferry service would cease at the end of the year. However, the line saw unusual activity in September when a number of steam-hauled trains were operated.

Thought worthy of comment in the early 1990s were the facts that the first all-female permanent way (PW) gang was employed to maintain the tracks at Bristol East Depot and that an eighteen year old lady had gained a job at Gloucester operating a MAS signalling system, one of only two females so employed.

As well as new liveries appearing repaints meant that the old order was disappearing and by February only a handful of all Mk 2e and 2f carriages remained in blue and grey with all of the rest in Intercity livery.

Sector codes were announced from mid-year to cover all loco stock rather than just a small proportion that had been allocated to date. A large number of existing codes were deleted with many more introduced. Some appeared to introduce a real level of complexity to day to day operations, at least in theory as for example new code IBRA denoted Intercity Long Range diesel 47/4, minimum use and contained just two locos 47801/2.

A familiar sight in magazines of the time were pictures taken at the Leicester scrapyard of Vic Berry where a mountain of both loco and carriage bodies had been accrued. Sadly, most of the contents of the stack were destroyed in an overnight fire on March 9. An estimated 100 carriages were involved. Subsequently, the company ceased trading in June, the business being perhaps the most prolific receiver of diesel locomotives and Mark I coaching stock for dismantling.

The first stirrings of what was to become big business was the hiring of locomotives, in this case 20087 and 20138, initially to RFS Industries, a company based at Doncaster Works, who then sub-hired them to Channel Tunnel

The 1200v Bury electric service ceased in July to make way for the new tram line rendering with Class 504 EMUs redundant. M65456 is seen at Radcliffe in April 1991. Colour-Rail.com

24

Britain's Railways in the 1990s

1991

The condemnation of 56042 took many enthusiasts by surprise as it was half the age of most diesels operating at the time. It is seen here at Toton in June 1991, three months before withdrawal, although the graffiti suggests that it had not been in service in recent months. K Nuttall/Colour-Rail.com

Works Group for use at Cheriton. Other class members were sold or possibly leased by BREL to CFD Industries and shipped to France. The sale is questioned as most of the locos subsequently returned to the UK. Heading into preservation in the UK were a number of Class 50s including 50019/35. HST power cars 43167-70 appeared to have been stored, some for the second time.

Rarely recorded was the fact that Pacers were at the time regular visitors to Inverness, although not in passenger service. They usually reached the highland capital by being coupled to a service train but locked out of use and their journeys north were to have Leyland TL11 engines fitted, these having been removed from first-generation units which also made their way to Inverness. Units recorded as present in February were 141108 and 142076.

Possibly the first recorded visit of a Class 90 to the East Coast route in Scotland saw 90046 running ECS from Morpeth to Edinburgh on the stock of a Northumbrian rail cruise special. On September 26 a record attempt for a journey between Kings Cross and Edinburgh was made when 91012 plus six carriages completed the trip in 3hrs 29mins ➤

Class 303 303048 was restored to a livery akin to that carried when new and was captured on film soon after its repaint and is seen near Motherwell on June 22. T Owen/Colour-Rail.com

Britain's Railways in the 1990s

25

Class 50 50019 headed off to a life in preservation following its withdrawal on September 19. Six weeks earlier it looked fit and well at Newton Abbot. C Tretheway/Colour-Rail.com

at an average speed of 112.9mph. The maximum permitted speed was 140mph – achieved for 147 miles including the summit of Stoke bank.

A notable working was that of Electro Diesel 73110 which reached Peterborough on November 28 with an engineer's train from Basingstoke.

The great British weather delayed many trains when heavy snow fell on February 7 and found some of the 'new' traction wanting especially the East Coast Class 91s and also the Class 317 and 321 EMUs. One official explanation for widespread disruption lasting several days was that it was 'the wrong kind of snow' being dry/powdery in nature allowing it to be blown into traction motors and door mechanisms.

Two sheds – much beloved by enthusiast on depot bashes around the East Midlands, Shirebrook and Barrow Hill – closed on February 9 with staff from the latter being transferred to new facilities at Worksop. The major but usually impenetrable level five shed at Stratford closed its doors on March 31 although a running shed remained to carry out more minor maintenance tasks. Another 'big name' shed to close its doors was Gateshead on July 8 with Heaton taking on any residual work. Demolishing started in September on the long-closed shed at Finsbury Park.

A sign of the times was the closure of all except one railway line within Newport Docks making it hard to imagine that 30 years earlier it provided employment for around 20 shunting locos.

With less than half of the projected number of 158s built some observers were surprised to see units carrying the numbers 158901-10, but these were a dedicated batch for use by West Yorkshire PTE which clearly wanted them to be easily identified as theirs. Meanwhile the class was now appearing across the network with examples being allocated to Norwich and Cardiff in March and some already being employed on Trans Pennine duties. The refitting of the Pacers with Voith transmission was a continuing programme and the Class 143s, which had worked in the North East from new, started to be transferred to Cardiff. Class 456 EMUs were being delivered in quantity though none had entered service by mid-year, reportedly due to a problem with the driving position and no doubt related to a similar problem encountered with the 321s. The first 165, 165001 was officially handed over at Marylebone on May 14, coinciding with the new maintenance facility opening at Aylesbury.

Locomotives awaiting cutting up following withdrawal tended to remain stored at the shed where they last had a duty, but a number of Class 20s were noted at Stanton Gate in March while 08s and Class 45s remained stored in quantity at March. Old Oak was another storage location and a number of Class 50s were cut up on site by Coopers Metals. Despite its closure Stratford also had 20 residents awaiting cutting up in the same month.

With stock availability always tight, if a failure occurred creative thinking produced interesting workings on occasions. One such happening took place on July 20 when an HST set decided that it did not want to go from Leeds to St Pancras. A substitute was provided from Sheffield in the shape of 156429 with it being the first of its type seen at the terminus. As it substituted for an eight-car HST it could best be described as 'well loaded'. Unexpected sightings could however have been planned to happen such as the regular summer Saturday appearance of Class 86 electrics at Great Yarmouth. These appeared as a result of through trains from Liverpool Street, with the electric loco being left attached from Norwich with the train being hauled by a Class 47/8.

An interesting initiative by the Coal sector was the organising of a running day between Crewe and Llandudno. All trains were double-headed with pairs of 20s, 37s, 56s, 58s and 60s involved.

Some once common railway activities just slipped away over time, one such being the deployment of bankers which were employed on almost every train at some locations in the steam era such as Exeter St Davids to Exeter Central. However such an event was noted as very much a rarity when on April 26 47635 on an engineer's train had to be assisted up the 1 in 37 bank by 33008/65.

A spectacular incident occurred on May 16 when an oil train became derailed at Bradford on Tone between Exeter and Taunton. Some of the fuel leaking from damaged tankers ignited and the subsequent heat then caused other tanks to explode. As well as the track damage and wreckage to clear all of the signalling cables were destroyed and restoration took five days during which time a limited service was maintained via the Yeovil-Exeter route.

Health and safety caught up with Scotrail's Class 158s which were designed to offer a catering service as well as carry bicycles. Plans for the refreshment trolley and bikes to be stored in the same

A magnet for many enthusiasts on a weekend shed bash was Shirebrook Junction. At first housing 47s it was best known for hosting a number of Class 56s but by the time of its closure it was 58s that predominated. 58022 plus others rested there on a Sunday in 1990. T Owen/Colour-Rail.com

1991

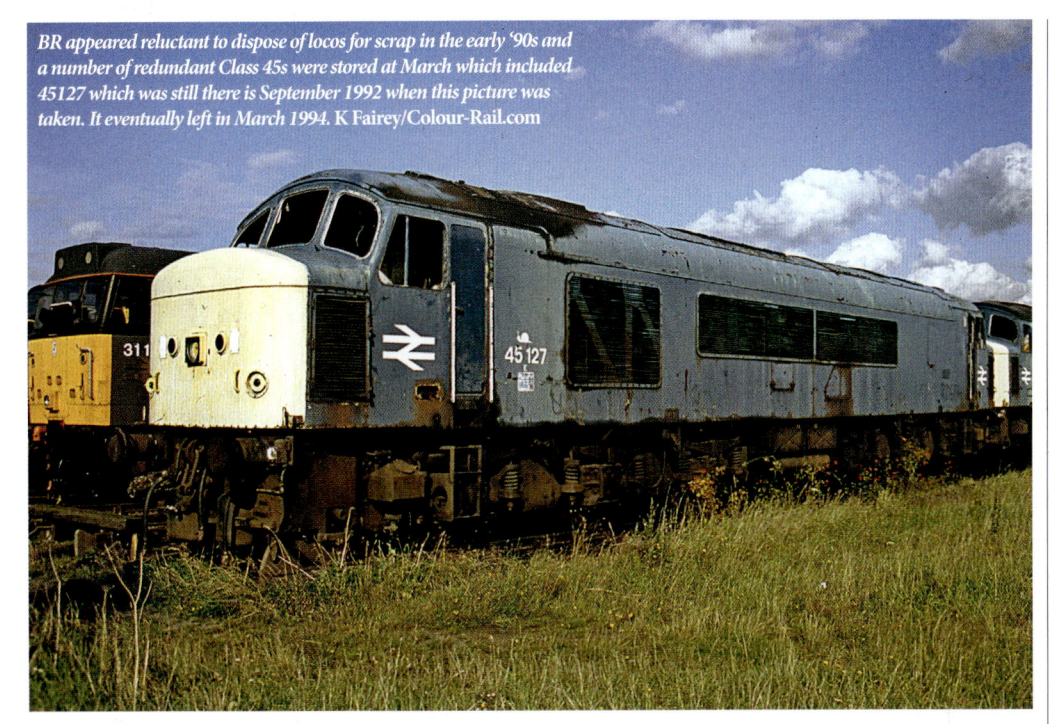

BR appeared reluctant to dispose of locos for scrap in the early '90s and a number of redundant Class 45s were stored at March which included 45127 which was still there is September 1992 when this picture was taken. It eventually left in March 1994. K Fairey/Colour-Rail.com

area were deemed unacceptable and no bikes could be carried on the Scotrail Express network which was exclusively worked by the 158s. More unwelcome was the tightening of rules and regulations at Doncaster works which stopped enthusiast visits at the end of the year.

Changing times were illustrated on summer Saturday services in Cornwall. All were worked by DMUs or HSTs, except for the up and down sleeper balanced by a Paddington-Penzance and return, plus an overnight Manchester-Penzance train returning at 10.18. All three duties were worked by Class 47s. The closure or lack of maintenance facilities caused large amounts of unproductive running in some cases. A case in point was the newly introduced Edinburgh to Poole HST, which during its supposed overnight sojourn at Bournemouth actually ran empty coach stock (ECS) to London and back for servicing. Fortunately a little more common sense prevailed at Hereford where carriage cleaning facilities were re-instated so that HSTs stabling overnight did not have to run to Bristol for cleaning.

Heritage

The Kent & East Sussex Railway entered the 100,000 visitors in a year club when it declared its passenger figures for 1990. The Mid Hants Railway also celebrated record visitor numbers. The Bluebell Railway issued a prospectus to encourage contributions needed, exceeding £1m, for the laying of the three and a half mile extension through Kingscote for the line to come within two miles of East Grinstead.

The Great Central Railway was chosen for running in trials for 5029 *Nunney Castle* which was fresh from overhaul at Didcot with the intention that it would see mainline use in the autumn. The first phase of planned work on the new Leicester North station was completed and the station was opened on July 5 as part of celebrations on the line to mark the 150th anniversary of the first 'excursion train' organised by one Thomas Cook

A Rail Day at Llandudno saw a number of visiting locos and shuttle trains run including this pair of Class 20s with 20163 leading. Colour-Rail.com

Britain's Railways in the 1990s

27

The scrapyard belonging to Vic Berry in Leicester had become famous for its stacks of carriages and loco bodies but a major fire there saw the yard close down in mid-year. In May 1990 Class 31 31259 was awaiting its fate. It did not end up in the pyramid and was cut up just a few weeks later. Colour-Rail.com

which ran from a station in Campbell Street, Leicester.

The Avon Valley Railway, a new entrant to the heritage market, opened for business on March 29 running trains from Bitton to Oldland Common and another start-up was the 15-in gauge Kirklees Light Railway which ran for one mile along the track bed of the Clayton West branch starting at that station. The Dart Valley Railway changed its name to the South Devon Railway opening for the season over the Easter weekend.

An ambitious plan was launched to build a brand new steam engine, this being an A1 pacific with roadshows to promote the project being held in London and Edinburgh.

The Llangollen Railway continued track laying west from Deeside Halt towards Glyndyfrdwy with the stated intention of reaching Corwen by 1996 and the Gloucestershire Warwickshire line was also heading west, its next

The Kent & East Sussex Railway reached one of its long term goals in the year with its re-opening of Bodiam station. The revived site looked a lot more pristine than it had in BR days when it was visited by a railtour hauled by A1X 32678 on October 19, 1958. Colour-Rail.com

Britain's Railways in the 1990s

1991

section being to Far Stanley and the Shackerstone Railway had a date of late 1991 to open a one and a half-mile extension from Market Bosworth to Shenton. Meanwhile, the East Lancashire Railway opened its extension, from Ramsbottom to Rawtenstall on April 26. Yet another extension was recorded on the Isle of Wight with track laying completed from Ashey to Smallbrook Junction with the line opening on July 20. Yet another extension was that at the Dean Forest Railway from Lydney Town to Lydney Riverside.

Heritage lines had started experimenting with diesel galas and the West Somerset Railway was perhaps the first line to run one without any 'support' from steam. Included in the line-up was D1010 in the guise of D1035 *Western Yeoman* making its debut on passenger duties. Other diesel developments had seen the arrival of the first DMU cars at the Severn Valley Railway.

Extensions to existing lines along with new heritage railways opening were a feature of the early 1990s. One start-up was the Kirklees Railway and loco 2-6-2T Fox is pictured there in July 1992. The loco, built in 1987, was nearly as new as the railway. Colour-Rail.com

Optimism has always been rife in the preservation movement, particularly when it comes to locomotive restoration and the owners of West Country 34010 *Sidmouth* and BR Standard 2-6-0 76077 were both predicting 'early steaming dates' for their charges, something that neither had achieved by the end of 2022.

Steam traction returned to the Cambrian Coast line with 7819 *Hinton Manor* and Standard 4MT being the rostered motive power with the first train running on June 16.

70000 *Britannia* joined the pool of registered main line engines. With all of the recent additions this period probably represented the largest number of engines available for main line duties of any in the preservation era.

The Tanfield railway continued to expand with the opening to Causey Arch taking place on August 15 with a further mile to East Tanfield planned for 1992. A large number of locos, carriages and wagons awaited restoration in the yard at Tanfield. Another line extending was the North Downs Railway with public services commencing on May 14.

A sign of what was to come was a directive from the Railway Inspectorate to the Severn Valley Railway to ban the public from entering the shed, workshops and loco yard at Bridgnorth.

Participants on steam-hauled mainline railtours were being 'sent to jail' as all stock used on those duties by BR was to receive window bars and have the opening lights restricted in movement. This was perhaps a little ironic as some modern traction enthusiast travelling on timetabled trains were noted for hanging their whole body out of carriage windows.

What was thought to be a first for a heritage line was the arrival by road of a locomotive from BRs capital stock this being Class 73, 73126 which was to be named after the line it was visiting, the Kent & East Sussex Railway, its arrival being on May 22. Its stay was brief departing again on 26th.

Peak Rail commenced running services from Darley Dale to a temporary platform at Matlock in mid-December. Their Buxton site still retained items of rolling stock but was officially described as 'mothballed'.

The much-anticipated return to steam of 60532 *Blue Peter* with a formal ceremony on December 11. It was then transferred temporarily by road to the North Yorkshire Moors Railway where it was tested and used briefly in service before returning to its maintenance base at ICI Wilton. ∎

The West Somerset Railway was one of the first to venture into the diesel gala market, but it did so in 1991 and hired in a Western owned by Yeomans, this being D1010 but in the guise of D1035 Western Yeoman. It was the first time the loco had been used on passenger services. It is seen here in 1989 when it visited the Didcot Railway Centre. Colour-Rail.com

Britain's Railways in the 1990s

29

Class 165 DMUs were put into service from Paddington replacing Class 117s, some of which found a new home in Scotland. 165116 was seen at Oxford on July 21. D Pye/Colour-Rail.com

1992

DECLINING FATE OF FREIGHT

The previous year had seen the start of the abolition of the railway's regional structure, completed in April when the last region, the Midland, was formally disbanded.

Work began on remodelling the layout and signalling at Paddington which would see many platform closures in the coming months. Class 165 turbo units were scheduled to take over some duties at the May timetable change. Another line being upgraded was the Waterloo & City where new stock was expected in 1992.

In order to increase capacity on some suburban lines around London First Class accommodation was temporarily removed, a case in point being the LTS section. Subsequently, it was announced that this would be made permanent as there were only 300 First Class season ticket holders, but seat provision was for around 1600 per day.

Initiatives in the freight sector often seemed to struggle and one such was Charterail which was formed in 1990 with BR holding a 22% stake. It ceased operations in mid-year.

At this time Royal Mail were still strongly committed to using rail to move letters and parcels and drew up plans for a new terminus near Willesden adjacent to the North Circular Road.

There were once again rumblings about replacing Birmingham New Street with this time a site at Aston being proposed. New Street was to remain but have only six platforms handling local services. A scheme that had been waiting approval was that for the opening of the Ivanhoe line from Leicester to Burton, this including no fewer than 16 new stations with work due to start in 1993.

Perhaps with a view towards the looming privatisation of the rail industry the government reviewed the amount payable to apply for a Light Railway Order with a proposal to raise the base payment from £50 to £750. That might have sounded inflationary but the £50 rate had been unchanged since 1896! Talks were about to start on applications for non-rail industry companies to run passenger services and first in line was Richard Branson with his new company Virgin Rail. Proving that life for private enterprise could be challenging, the Stagecoach overnight service to and from Scotland was withdrawn due to poor patronage.

As might have been predicted, work on the Channel Tunnel did not keep up with the schedule and the planned opening in June 1993 was postponed with a 12-month delay anticipated. However, Metro Cammell was instructed to start work on building the 139 vehicles

Stagecoach embarked on a short lived experiment to provide Mk2d carriages on sleeper services from Scotland, this lasting less than 12 months. One of the small fleets is seen at Aberdeen. P Chancellor/Colour-Rail.com

1992

required to provide the planned overnight services from across the UK. Those services were scheduled to start in mid-1995. Another delay, this time of six months, was announced for the delivery of the Class 92s, said to be due to 'a technical problem'. A number of locomotives owned by German state railway DB were employed on duties at Cheriton.

An extension to the London Underground system for the Jubilee line from Green Park to Stratford was under discussion in parliament in January.

Passenger numbers in many areas were booming and the north of Scotland was no exception with income on the lines doubling in the last three years, this contributing to Scotrail being the most successful Regional Railways profit centre.

Opening dates were announced for the Manchester Metrolink with Bury being reached in April, Altrincham in May, and Piccadilly in July but the third remained out of use at the end of July. A ten-minute frequency service was operating between Bury and Altrincham. The Tyne Wear Metro announced plans to extend the system to Sunderland, subject to council backing and appropriate funding.

A relatively new feature of UK power generation was the use of imported coal rather than using the home mined variety. With relevance to present day challenges the year saw the import of a large consignment of coal from Russia in September which used rail transport from the docks to the power stations.

Maintenance provision was evolving all the time as the re-organised railway sought value for money rather than just sending locos to their traditional works. Traction and rolling stock maintenance and repair company RFS Industries at Kilnhurst were active in the market and provided a full overhaul for 09005 which was seen at Doncaster on March 8. In a similar vein, Landore shed won a contract to repaint ten RES Class 47s, and Glasgow Works was regularly repairing West Coast electrics with six being present during a visit made in February. Crewe Works was only giving classified repairs to 08 shunters although mainline locomotives did arrive for one-off repairs. A visit in July found just two engines receiving attention.

A subject from the 1980s reared its head again, this being the proposal to build Worcester Parkway station. To say that BR was not enthusiastic seemed an understatement– prevarication and delays would ensure it was another 28 years before the station opened.

On February 28, the IRA bombed London Bridge station. Twenty-three people were injured and all the capital's termini were closed for most of the day. The next month, on March 9, a device exploded in a control cabinet near Wandsworth Common causing more disruption.

The use of steam power on BR came to an end with the withdrawal of the last steam crane, ADRS95000 built in 1955.

The proposed Midlands Metro suffered a setback when the government deferred a £300m grant for at least 12 months.

Perhaps not evident to the casual observer were the implications of sectorisation with every asset being sector allocated. That included engine sheds and possibly sealing its fate in years to come was the transfer of Bristol Bath Road solely to the Intercity sector and so just having Class 47s to look after. Cardiff Canton however became exclusively a Regional Railways depot.

Network South East planned to impose a smoking ban on all of its services from the start of 1993.

Stock changes

Gaining an accurate picture of locomotive deliveries, allocations and withdrawals was becoming increasingly challenging, firstly with the official annual returns not being published until many months after the financial year end, but also the monthly changes notified by BR not bearing a great deal of resemblance to what was being recorded by enthusiasts. The official annual return, dated March 31, showed that locomotive stock reduced from 2227 in 1991 to 2096 in 1992. Classes 08 and 47 had seen the largest reductions although Class 60 numbers had increased from 21 to 86.

In an unusual move the new Class 159 cars were to be built at Derby to the Class 158 design and then sent to Rosyth Royal Dockyard for the installation of first class accommodation and a revised cab access amongst other changes. All units were scheduled for completion by the year end. When released from Derby works each carried a 1588XX unit number, being renumbered on completion at Rosyth, the first such being noted at Bristol on July 14. 465001 was delivered to the Southern on January 19. The total number of sets on order was 100 being 465001-50 and 465201-50, units in these two series being delivered simultaneously from

Tram operations resumed on the streets of Manchester during the year and one of the first is seen at Manchester Victoria. Colour-Rail.com

On display at what appears to be an open day at Bournemouth West depot was new 465006 on September 12. The unit had not yet entered service and indeed for this class that turned out to be quite a protracted process. D Pye/Colour-Rail.com

Britain's Railways in the 1990s 31

York and Metro Cammell. The first units entered service on October 11 after the unveiling of Class 323 with a photo call for 323201 on September 25. Optimism prevailed around the Crossrail project with the announcement of rolling stock plans, these being for four-car electric multiple units (EMUs) designated as Class 341, based on the current Networker design – 138 units were thought to be required. Orders would not be placed until 1994 but the first services were to begin in early 1997. With the completion of the Mk IV carriage orders, no further hauled coaching stock – other than for Channel Tunnel use – was on order. It was a situation that was to persist for nearly 30 years.

It might have been thought that the condemnation of Class 56 56042 in 1991 was a 'one off', presumably due to the loco being damaged, but when 56017 (May) and 56002 (July) were condemned it appeared that the life of the class members might become much shorter than originally anticipated. 56122 joined the condemned list in October. A notable condemnation in August was of the experimental electric 89001. However, it would return to the network in due course. Two new sub class was created with the start of a small conversion programme for Class 08 to 09/1 and 09/2 with 09101 being created from 08833, the difference in sub class being dependent on the electrical system employed on the original locos. The main difference between an 08 and an 09 was the maximum speed which for an 09 was 27mph.

An outbreak of 'internationalism' became evident with the repainting of 90128-30 in SNCB, DB and SNCF liveries respectively and these were exhibited at the 'Freightconnection 92' exhibition at the NEC together with a French locomotive brought over specially by sea to Middlesbrough and then by road.

A well-known landmark was removed at the end of August when the remaining iron work of Clapham Junction A signal box that spanned the tracks beyond the London end of the station was dismantled.

It would seem that generic problems with rolling stock have always plagued the industry. All of the Pacer fleet had received reliability modifications, but unit shortages continued with some 15 cancellations daily in the Merseyside area and heritage unit substitutions elsewhere. The driving van trailers (DVTs) on the West Coast line were all being modified leading to services from Euston to Birmingham being worked in conventional mode. The whole 158 fleet had to receive modification to equipment racks following the discovery of fatigue cracks. The shortage of this type even saw Class 58s deployed with coaching stock on some Birmingham-Cambridge duties.

Conversions of Class 155 cars to 153 saw a substantial number arrive by the start of the year, which combined with all of the Class 158 deliveries, caused perhaps the greatest changes in diesel multiple unit (DMU) duties across all except the Southern area as many 156s were cascaded with knock on moves for most other types, of course the underlying aim being to remove both loco hauled passenger duties and first generation DMUs from service. The 153s were due to be introduced to the Central Wales line from May, the prospect being met with consternation by the locals as both seating capacity and bicycle carrying facilities would be reduced. Bath Road, Landore and Canton had been responsible for maintain heritage DMUs but all the work was concentrated at Canton from March. Despite the increased allocation all heritage DMUs were removed from Cardiff Valley duties. Likewise, the arrival of around 80 Class 60s had seen the 56s demoted from front line duties which in theory should have had a major impact on the number of Class 47s used on freight duties. Another effect of the new arrivals was the elimination of Class 20 duties in their spiritual home of the East Midlands. Twenty-two were noted in the vicinity of Toton depot with most being out of use.

Also noted was the fact that First Generation DMUs were still receiving overhauls with a Class 101 unit being seen returning to Scotland from a visit to Doncaster Works. Indeed, there appeared to be increased demand for them as Scotrail required an additional ten 2-car sets to work planned new services. That said, a large programme of withdrawals was under way although many of the condemned cars were the displaced Class 115s that had operated out of Marylebone where the final day of use was July 29. Canton lost all of its heritage allocation at the end of September with some going to Newton Heath for further use. Use of such sets in the Sheffield area also came to an end, at least in theory, as none were contracted to PTE sponsored services, but that did not stop them being rostered on long distance Regional Railway services. It might have been expected that with the arrival of Class 165s for duties out of Paddington the Class 117 DMUs would be sent for scrap, but a large quantity were to be refurbished and retained even finding their way to Scotland.

The arrival of the final batch of Mk IV carriages ended production of loco-hauled carriages in the UK except those intended for channel tunnel use. The production line, seen here at Crewe, would soon fall silent. R Hunter/Colour-Rail.com

Class 09 locos had been around since the 1960s but it seemed that in the '90s there was a need for additional members of the class, leading to the conversion of a small number of 08s to classes 09/1 and 09/2. One such was 08831 which became 09102 seen less than three weeks after emerging as such at Crewe on October 7. John E Henderson/Colour-Rail.com

1992

London Underground took delivery of the first of many new trains for the Central line in May.

Just three Class 50s remained in stock at the end of May and worked an official last duty between Salisbury and Exeter.

Services

Maesteg-Cardiff passenger services started from September 28 although two new stations were not ready in time, these being at Maesteg Ewenny Road and Bridgend Wind Mill. The popularity of the new service saw trains strengthened, extras being run and some would-be passengers being conveyed by bus.

The industry was giving out mixed messages in respect of its interest in growing the freight market announcing the closure of the Freightliner depot at Bristol West which had been handling 18,000 containers per year. Willesden and Gushetfaulds FLTs were also closed. One freight flow that was apparently still buoyant was that of Rover cars with five trains per day being scheduled.

Retrenchment on Cross Country passenger duties saw most of the services that had run to Poole being cut back to Bournemouth. Elsewhere a number of services from Shrewsbury were extended to Birmingham International to terminate to save space at New Street, a practice that remains today. Another trend that was gathering pace was the introduction of long through journeys and the title for the longest Sprinter duty seemed to be vested in the 11.45 Penzance-Milford Haven, a journey of 366.5 miles calling at 41 stations and taking in excess of eight hours.

A new service to commence with the May timetable change was that from Middlesbrough to Liverpool and it was hoped it would further increase Trans Pennine travel which had doubled in the last five years.

The future of Southampton boat trains was a subject for debate following the decline in both the number of ships calling and the decimation of the rail system within the docks. However, a train was provided on May 29 when the *Canberra* visited. Comprising just a Class 33 and 4TC unit even this short formation was described as 'lightly loaded'.

A favourite scheme was given a dust-off for consideration yet again, that being the running of network services from Taunton to the West Somerset Railway on a daily basis. On this occasion a 'park and ride' facility was suggested for Bishops Lydeard.

The demise of the excursion train was notable with some of the big rugby matches that might have had up to 15 specials provided in the '60s and '70s not having. Another major event, the Spalding Flower festival, attracted just four trains in 1992.

Passenger services resumed on May 11 between Wakefield and Knottingley with three new stations provided. Class 141 units provided the service.

The northeast of England had the honour of hosting the last unfitted freight trains on BR, these consisting of Covhop wagons conveying Alumina from North Blyth to Lynemouth Alcan works.

Following Nationalisation in 1948 there was a concerted drive to remove private owner wagons from the system. Perhaps illustrating how things had nearly gone full circle a report revealed that there were in excess of 85 companies owning wagons at the start of 1992 totalling 13640 wagons. However, that was well exceeded by the in excess of 16,000 vehicles allocated to engineering departments.

The Kings Lynn electrification scheme was completed in

With the arrival of the Class 60s the end appeared nigh for many older locos including the Class 20s although ultimately they demonstrated a strong survival instinct. Many withdrawn examples were to be seen stored in and around Toton as seen here on October 17. S R Lee/Colour-Rail.com

Class 90s 90128-30 were treated to the application of the liveries of the French, German and Belgian railways and 90130 is seen in its new guise passing through Crewe on October 7. John E Henderson/Colour-Rail.com

The Class 115 DMUs, for long the providers of all of the suburban trains from Marylebone, had reached their sell by date and upon arrival of the Class 165s they were consigned to the scrap heap. Their duties ended in mid-1992. Colour-Rail.com

August with the service from Kings Cross taken over by Class 317s from on the 22nd.

Operations

From January 20, trains from Marylebone to Banbury were increased in frequency to run at one per hour. Illustrating the important part that coal played in railway finances, five coal trains were observed in just over four hours at Banbury hauled by Class 58s. A further coal train had Class 60 power as did two oil counterparts.

Today's diet of intermodal services did not feature. Wandsworth appeared to be another 'loco hot spot' with 17 being noted in under four hours on March 30.

The previously announced ban on services calling at unlit stations halted after dark calls at many stations on the Cambrian line as BR stated it did not have the funds to provide lighting. The safety concern was laudable, but the fact that Central Wales line trains could call at such stations because it was classed as a 'light railway' made no sense at all. Llandrindod became the only staffed station on the line from the start of the winter timetable.

Life in a world without mobile phones was experienced in East Anglia when, due to a unit failure, passengers were stuck aboard for two hours. The guard collected home phone numbers from some passengers so that control could ring them to advise of the delay.

At Leamington the partial collapse of a viaduct to the south of the station saw single line working introduced and many cross country services terminating short. Full reinstatement of the structure was expected to take three months and the track was expected to take three weeks to re-open.

A three-year track upgrade project began on the Forth Bridge. When built, instead of the use of sleepers two metal troughs, one and three-quarter miles in length, were laid which contained lengths of hardwood. A unique design of wide bottom rail was then secured to the wood. 150 years later and supplies of the rails were running out and it was decided to replace the hardwood

Three Class 50s clung to life for 'special duties' after the rest of the class were withdrawn. On April 4 50033 and 50050 were employed on the Hoovering Druid tour which took them from Derby deep into South Wales and the pair are seen on the outward leg of the tour near Stoke Works. R Siviter/Colour-Rail.com

1992

Class 317 EMUs had been a familiar sight at Kings Cross for a number of years but with the completion of the electrification through to Kings Lynn they gained new duties in 1992. 317s in bulk were to be seen at Kings Cross in August 1989. D Pye/Colour-Rail.com

which was now placed on rubber cushions and then with the use of specially designed fixing plates conventional rails could be used.

Reminiscent of a St Trinian's film, an outbreak of fisticuffs involving an estimated 150 schoolgirls broke out at Wimbledon station on April 7. The police made several arrests – taking them 'down the station' on a commandeered London bus.

Partly to promote their good performance Network South East published data at Reading that showed in a 16-week period they had achieved a score of 98.7% for reliability and 85.2% on time performance against a target of 80%. The downside was that they would be using the figures going forward to refund season ticket holders if targets were not met.

Local knowledge always comes in handy when looking for timetabling anomalies. It had long been the practice to insert two or three minutes' recovery time into schedules approaching the place where a train terminated. Nonetheless, East Coast planners excelled with the 09.00 service from Kings Cross being allowed 84 minutes for the final 57 miles of its journey compared with the 09.30 train that faced a massive 64 minutes to travel the 29 miles from Dunbar.

North Berwick line trains had settled down to use almost exclusively cascaded Class 305 units. One of these units made a surprise appearance at Glasgow Central on February 22 when it was used on a railtour organised by BR which took it to Ayr before running from there through to North Berwick creating many other 'firsts' along the way. The class was also breaking new ground in Manchester being allocated to Hadfield duties replacing Class 304s.

The East Coast route was regularly seeing trains worked by Class 90s with up to three usually on hire. However, the honour of hauling the first electric hauled postal service from Newcastle fell to 91024.

The industry was trying hard to promote itself and BR open days were planned at Doncaster, Haymarket, Kings Lynn, Worcester, Eastleigh and Springs Branch during the year. One not on the list was Aylesbury where the new Chiltern depot hosted two Deltics and a number of BR diesel types on April 25.

A Class 91 saw use on the West Coast mainline when 91029 was provide for a record attempt between Manchester and Euston on April 30. The time recorded was 128 minutes and three seconds. On its return it passed Birmingham International from Euston in just under 64 minutes. Another record was set, this time between Glasgow and Edinburgh on May 6 with 158708/10 making the trip in 32 minutes.

With the demise of Vic Berry's scrapyard at Leicester there were new entrants to the railway scrap market with Gwent Demolition operating at Margam and MC Metals adjacent to Glasgow Works, Amongst others active were Booth Roe Metals at Rotherham and Coopers Metals at Attercliffe.

An observer at Newcastle recorded the first visit of a Class 87 to the city on August 15 when 87027 appeared hauling an HST power car.

A formal 'end of era' celebration took place at Paddington when 47431 worked 'the last locomotive hauled train', this actually relating to the Thames Valley commuter services which went over to Class 165/1 operation. Daytime locomotive haulage on the Edinburgh-Inverness route also ended with 47671/4 employed on the last day, September 26.

A loco failure saw the unprecedented sight of a passenger train headed by five locomotives when August 23 a Class 86 failed near Diss with four Class 90s, which just happened to be running light engine in the area, coming to the rescue.

Station improvements were announced for the Salisbury-Exeter line ahead of the arrival of the Class 159 units and work had started on building the new

A clutch of Class 305 units made redundant on duties out of Liverpool Street found new employment far from their old home. Some maintained the Edinburgh-East Berwick service, but others such as 305510 shown here, replaced Class 303s on the run from Manchester Piccadilly to Hadfield. D Pye/Colour-Rail.com

High-speed trains had long been in command of long distance services from Paddington, but some rush hour commuter services continued to employ Class 47s on hauled stock but the end came during 1992. 47431 which hauled the official last train, is seen here approaching the terminus on April 23. D Pye/Colour-Rail.com

It wasn't just diesel locomotives that were being retired. 62660 Butler Henderson *reached the end of its boiler ticket and bowed out on the Great Central Railway. It is seen here at Swithland on February 20. C J Gammell/Colour-Rail.com*

depot at Salisbury. The use of Class 50s on the route continued to dwindle as their number in service approached single figures. However, their temporary replacements, the 47/7s appeared to continue to provide availability challenges.

The first part of the Birmingham Cross City line from Lichfield to New Street went live from 30 November. However, as the section south from Birmingham was not ready and some through services were planned, limited DMU usage was retained on the Northern section and the EMUs used were from classes 304 and 310 rather than the new 323s.

Enthusiasts who 'enjoyed a good walk' as part of their day out 'spotting' were disappointed to learn of the closure of Platform 11 at Manchester Victoria, once the longest platform in the country.

The railway continued to reap the benefits of modernisation. If loss of adhesion due to leaf fall was a problem, it worsened each season, in part as vegetation encroached along the track side but primarily because so many units were not using clasp brakes, the application of which removed the leaf 'gunge' from the tyres.

As seen many times in this publication, hindsight is a wonderful thing- this time in respect of lineside vegetation when a proposal to remove trees from the trackside for two and a half miles east from Salisbury station brought loud protests from residents. Failure to clear the trees on this section of line in 2021 was the major contributor to the accident at Salisbury where on train slid into another on the slippery leaf mulch that covered the rails.

A large programme of platform extensions were under way in the southeast to accommodate the new Networker trains with some 30 stations affected.

An unusual prosecution for indecency occurred in August, following a young couple 'making love' in a crowded carriage, it apparently only becoming an issue when one of them lit a cigarette in the non-smoking coach.

Another depot to fall from grace was Eastfield which stopped maintenance in August and closed at the end of September. As one of its final acts it turned out 26007/1 as D5300/1 in original style green livery. Motherwell was to take on some of the work, but such was the set-up of the Sectors that Scotrail operated Petroleum sector 37s had to travel to Immingham for any heavy maintenance.

In recent years many locomotives that had been named had received 'stainless steel' plates with cast plates fitted to HSTs being replaced with the steel variety. It seemed that cast plates were now back in fashion when the railway press stated that 91025, which was named *BBC Radio One FM* at Kings Cross on September 30, would be the last to utilise the steel design plates.

In a sign of the times, Crewe works gained a contract for the overhaul of just the power units from classes 37, 43 and 47 that were sent to the works by road or rail. The once mighty works saw its ownership move from BREL to ABB Transportation, the group also owning the carriage works at Derby. Laira, Selhurst and Neville Hill were among depots carrying out heavy repairs. Doncaster may have been the most active of the former BR works at this time with around 30 locos present. Freight service handlers RFS won a new contract to prepare Class 20s for use on Channel Tunnel duties, these numbering 20 by the year end with no fewer than five of them coming from heritage lines 'preserved' stock.

Our changing industrial heritage was noted with the closure of the Ravenscraig steelworks in July, which had been a major user of the railway system. The year seemed to be characterised by 'last freight trains' as various facilities – many of them coal mines – closed or moved to road transport for their needs.

Up until the end of November the weather seemed to have been

The Tanfield Railway completed its planned extension to the west by reaching Tanfield East during the year! Working on this section of the line was 0-6-0ST No. 22 in 1994. P Chancellor/Colour-Rail.com

1992

Running of mainline steam over former Southern lines that had third rail electrification had long been resisted by BR. The first chink in their armour saw 34027 *Taw Valley* work from Waterloo to Bournemouth under cover of darkness to deter trespassers.

The Battlefield line opened through to Shenton on August 2 double headed by 0-4-0ST *Linda* and 0-4-0 WT *The King*.

A less well-known preservation project was the creation of the Scapa Flow Light Railway on the Orkney island of Hoy which appeared almost overnight when 100 yards of track was laid in two days by volunteers from Scotrail. An opening ceremony was held on September 20. The only motive power was a three-cylindered Ruston & Hornsby diesel and there was no rolling stock at the line. Another low-profile project was the Vobster Light Railway but actually based at Mells between Frome and Radstock.

One of the less pleasant sides of preservation occasionally reared its head, this being theft of components, either for scrap value or occasionally perhaps for use elsewhere. One such was a replacement firebox removed from the Blaenavon Big Pit museum.

On October 11, the Tanfield Railway extension opened from Causey Arch to East Tanfield.

The Crewe Heritage Centre changed its name to The Railway Age during the year to focus on modern traction rather than steam power.

Heritage line steam loco stock was increased by one when USA designed S160 2253 arrived at Tees dock from Poland on October 27 and was in steam at The North Yorkshire Moors railway four days later.

particularly benign but on the 30th severe flooding of lines in the West Country and Wales led to much disruption, lasting in some places for a full week.

Heritage

The Welshpool and Llanfair Railway was constructing a new station at Welshpool Raven Square using a building previously at Eardisley with a planned opening at Easter. The original terminus of the line disappeared under a ring road roundabout.

60532 *Blue Peter* made its main line debut in March and 4771 *Green Arrow* came to the end of its mainline duties in August.

West Country 34007 *Wadebridge* transferred by road from the Plym Valley Railway to the Bodmin & Wenford line becoming the heaviest engine ever to traverse the Saltash bridge.

The Heritage movement started to provide services for the national system with the Midland Railway Centre gaining a contract to repaint ten carriages for Regional Railways.

One of the rare instances of identity swaps (at the time) of engines in use on mainline duties saw 34027 *Taw Valley* carry 34028 on one cabside and M7 30053 appear as 30673 when working at Salisbury and June 28.

Engines recently steamed following restoration included Jinty 47327 at Butterley, S15 847 at the Bluebell and GWR 2-6-0 7325 at the Severn Valley Railway while 62660 *Butler Henderson* was retired at the Great Central on February 24. On the move to a new home was 16XX pannier tank 1638 swapping Devon for Kent to work on the Kent & East Sussex Railway.

The Llangollen Railway was operating through to Glyndyfrdwy from the start of the season with some former wooden buildings from Northwich shed being erected there. Also extended was the Bluebell Railway with three miles of track added to reach New Coombe Bridge.

An additional heritage attraction was the Steeple Grange Railway being a narrow gauge line with a short length of track laid at Steeplehouse Junction on the trackbed of the Cromford and High Peak line near Wirksworth.

With the supply of engines from Barry scrapyard exhausted, some preservationists looked further afield for serviceable locos. One arrival, via Tees dock from Poland, was USA S160 2253 which was quickly steamed at the North Yorkshire Moors Railway. Seen raising the echoes at Green End it was heading for Pickering on April 2 1996.
P Chancellor/Colour-Rail.com

Britain's Railways in the 1990s

The relative calm of Reading station was disrupted on October 24 when a bomb exploded close to the track closing the station for two days. No damage occurred to the station. All appears to be under control in this 1995 view with Turbo and EMU units awaiting their next turns of duty. K Fairey/Colour-Rail.com

1993

'SHEDS' GIVE WAY TO DEPOTS

Plans for privatisation continued to emerge with the South Western division of the Southern, Fenchurch Street-Southend and the East Coast mainline being early candidates for franchise agreements.

New legislation had been enacted in 1992 under the title Transport and Works Act. In perhaps an unexpected early use of its new powers, a train controller at Exeter St Davids was charged with being 'drunk in charge of a railway station'.

Bomb alerts continued to disrupt services, particularly in the southeast. Fortunately attacks on the trains themselves were rare but on February 3 a device was placed on a Victoria to Ramsgate service. Following a telephoned warning the train was stopped at Kent House and evacuated before the bomb was detonated causing considerable damage to one carriage. A bomb outside Liverpool Street station on April 24 blew out around 25% of the glass in the newly restored station roof. Reading was cut off from the network on October 24/25 after a bomb exploded beside the track with permission to restart services not coming until late on the second day. The nearest any trains could get to the main station was the chord from the main line to Reading West. A number of other stations on the South West division were targeted on the same day.

Speculation was always rife about both potential line openings and closures with the Central Wales line again seen as under threat as subsidy funds were being cut. It was an issue that needed to be dealt with if full franchise operation of the network was to be achieved. One line thought to already be 'dead' was that on Weymouth Quay, but four special trains operated there on April 3.

Frodingham, perhaps one of the least mentioned sheds of the era closed at the end of March. Wakefield shed, which closed as such back in 1966, was subsequently used for wagon repairs but this too stopped and it was demolished during the year. The ever decreasing number of depots saw engines out-stationed at locations which were unexpected such as Petroleum sector Class 60s allocated to Immingham where two were always actually working from Eastleigh.

The smoking ban imposed by Network South East in 1992 started to spread with Bristol-Southampton and Weymouth trains designated smoker-free on April 1

Despite looming privatisation management seemed determined

Frodingham depot was perhaps an unlikely survivor into the 1990s, especially with Immingham being relatively close. Neither location seemed to attract the attention of photographers with any frequency. Despite the former's closure in 1993, it remained in use for storage of withdrawn engines and 47352 rested there in 1999. The loco had gone into store at the depot in July 1993 and was cut-up on the spot in May 2000. K Fairey/Colour-Rail

Britain's Railways in the 1990s

1993

to crack down on 'public disorder'. A justifiable target was fare dodging and a fixed £10 penalty was introduced for travelling without a ticket. Another target was 'misappropriation of trolleys' at Euston where a £1 deposit was introduced on luggage trolleys, aimed apparently at their use to St Pancras or Kings Cross. Another target was railway enthusiasts at Rugby and Coventry where notices appeared prohibiting 'train spotting', this move apparently being justified as part of a crime prevention initiative.

Some financial information provided by the railways could be called questionable. Dilton Marsh Halt between Westbury and Salisbury was said to need replacement at a cost of £200,000, a sum which neither BR nor the county council was prepared to spend. The local parish council obtained an estimate to repair the station to give a further ten years of use of £3,000. Ultimately an affordable compromise was reached with a cost of £50,000. On the Cambrian line maintenance was deferred due to lack of money and the production of local timetable leaflets was abandoned, the latter said to make a saving of £300,000! Another issue on the line was accidents at crossings, there being 26 in six months but it was noted that there were a total of 364 on the whole Cambrian system.

A proposal to extend the Tyne Wear Metro to Ashington was made but rejected on the grounds that the projected cost of £100m would not be justified by passenger loadings.

The freight terminals at Trafford Park and Wembley opened for business in the autumn. The provision of a station for Channel Tunnel services at Ashford was resolved when John Laing agreed to build it at no cost to the taxpayer in return for a payment for every passenger who used it.

The RFS works at Kilnhurst was closed during the year, this site having conducted the rebuilding programme for Class 09 and the preparation of Class 20 locos for Channel Tunnel duties. As a result the company's site at Doncaster was used to store the Class 20s that had been returned from Channel Tunnel use by mid-year. Those hired from preservation groups returned directly to their owners in the spring.

Illustrating the death throes of the UK coal industry was the closure of Westoe and Easington collieries leaving just two operational in the whole of the North East.

Intercity was the best performing passenger business sector with freight receipts and property sales also making sizeable contributions. The shape of the post privatisation railway also became clearer with a total of 25 passenger franchises proposed. There were also proposals for the leasing of locomotives with three leasing companies being suggested with one having classes 86 and 91, another 43 (part) and 47, and the third would take 43 (the rest), 73/2, 87 and 90. Classes such as the 08s and 37s were not mentioned. Crucially the responsibility for the track was to be invested in a new government-owned company to be known as Railtrack. Its primary responsibilities were set out along with the principle that its activities would be financed by the operators paying track access charges. Despite a workforce of 12,500 it was anticipated that all of the track maintenance work would be contracted out, initially to companies within the BR organisation, but with the expectation that these in turn would move into the private sector. Railtrack, as owner of stations and depots would lease these to the operating companies. Timetabling, train planning and signalling would all be within scope as crucially would be health and safety.

60028, along with other Petroleum sector members of the class, was allocated to Immingham for maintenance but at least two of the class were out-stationed at Eastleigh, where this picture was taken on May 30. Colour-Rail.com

The first Class 92 to be released from the Brush Works at Loughborough was 92002. Subsequent works attention was occasionally provided by Crewe where the loco was seen on the traverser in 1996. Colour-Rail.com

Completing 35 years in traffic, the earliest members of Class 26 26001/2 had received a repaint in green a couple of years earlier. New to Hornsey shed as D5301, 26001 finished its days nominally allocated to Inverness and is seen at Edinburgh Waverley on August 14 shortly before withdrawal. K Fairey/Colour-Rail.com

The Railtrack safety regime would require approval by the Health and Safety Executive but then Railtrack would approve the safety cases of all of the operating companies.

An infrastructure item coming under Railtrack control was signalling. Despite a plethora of new schemes many semaphore signals remained in use and in former Great Northern areas even some somersault ones controlled the trains on a daily basis.

Once a major item of interest for some enthusiasts, the country's industrial railways had both dwindled in number and interest with some of those still going employing ex BR shunters rather than the more exotic fayre found in the 1960s and '70s. The Ministry of Defence, some coal board sites and even scrap yards were the focus of interest in the 1990s. Needless to say that those having military uses had to be viewed with a deal of discretion.

The next move in the preparation of the freight business saw the setting up of three companies, these to come into operation in April 1994, which would see the end of the sector era. They were roughly based on geographical areas with the North East company the most easily defined having all depots in northeast England and down to Doncaster under its wing. The South East company had control of Shirebrook, mentioned despite its recent closure, and then the former Eastern and Midland lines to the capital, part of the Western region with a new depot being constructed at Didcot, and all of the erstwhile Southern region. This left the West company the whole of Scotland, the West Coast Main Line, Wales and the western parts of the Western region although the only depots mentioned there were St Blazey and Gloucester.

Stock changes

The last of the new Class 60s were taken into stock soon after the start of the year, these not as might be expected 60098-60100 but 60007/9/13/6 in January and February with the final arrival being 60015 in March.

More Class 59s were placed on order, these being 59201-6 for National Power. The first Class 92 noted on the network was 92002 on December 10 when it was moved to Derby.

The end of the line came for Class 26 with the last eight examples being condemned in October, these having long outlasted the similar but later built Class 27s. The year was generally quite quiet in respect of loco withdrawals with Class 08 having the most casualties with odd members of classes 31 and 33 being included each month. However November brought attention back to the 56s, which following the 1992 casualties, had not featured in the condemnations but 56015/28/30 all went in that month with 56013/23 followed in December. The prevalence of the Romanian built examples (56001-30) will be noted.

The year on the former Southern region saw the arrival of both the first Class 159 and Class 466 units. Three Class 159s had been noted in service at Exeter by the end of March. In theory at least loco hauled services between Salisbury and Exeter ceased on July 10 although some diesel electric multiple unit (DEMU) duties remained on a temporary basis. Also new were Class 482 electric multiple units (EMUs), these being the replacement stock for the Waterloo and City line (W&C). As they were very similar to current London Underground stock they went to their West Ruislip depot for commissioning and trials. The situation with stock availability on the W&C was such that if any of the nine serviceable cars failed the system would need to close as passenger volumes could not be handled safely with any less.

Deliveries of Class 465s as well as 466 took place during the year with a new series 465/1 being seen towards the year end. The 166s were completed but some of the 323s were yet to see the light of day although entry into service of any of the class had again been delayed due to transformer explosions on two of the units. However with privatisation looming, rolling stock orders were about to dry

The year witnessed a complete change in the motive power provided for Waterloo-Exeter services. Having enjoyed Class 7 and 8 power in steam days they had continued to be worked by front line diesels from 1964, although they might not have always been on best form. Now loco hauled services were to be swept away by the arrival of the Class 159 units with a number seen at the new Salisbury depot. B Perryman/Colour-Rail.com

Britain's Railways in the 1990s

up and indeed the 166s were the last diesel units constructed until the arrival of the 168s towards the end of the decade with the lack of orders decimating the UK train building industry. Only the Heathrow Express and Skipton electrification schemes would offer any relief in the short term.

The first Class 373 unit, the stock for Channel Tunnel duties arrived in the UK via the tunnel on June 20 and soon took up residence at the new North Pole depot. The vast complexity of the project was appearing in the enthusiasts press and one wonders how it would have all come together if the UK services away from London had come to pass as stock for e.g. trains to Swansea was different for trains going to Scotland with no interchangeability. Even depot security would have made life difficult as sheds such as Laira and Landore would have taken on fortress style fencing etc. Each set was on an eight day cycle for maintenance and services to Plymouth and Swansea were envisaged as being worked by pairs of specially adapted Class 37s. Nine French state-owned SNCF locomotives had received modifications to allow them to work through the tunnel as far as Dollands Moor.

The 47/7 series of locomotives were originally designed for Push-Pull operation in Scotland and when those duties ceased they regularly worked the Waterloo-Exeter trains. Thus the appearance of more locos carrying 47/7 numbers caused some confusion but these were in a new series from 47721 upwards and in Res livery, these being fitted with long range fuel tanks.

A survey of high-speed train (HST) sets early in the year showed that there were 40 on the East Coast, Midland Main line and based away from the Western region for Cross Country services. The Western had 57 sets allocated including a number nominally for Cross Country duties but, for instance, the WR also supplied sets to work trains from Euston to Holyhead. Well over 100 sets of heritage DMUs remained in traffic.

With the influx of Networker units, a lot of the older Southern Rail electric multiple unit (EMU) types were heading for the scrap yard. The electro-pneumatic brake (EPB) type had a farewell tour on South London lines on May 14. Improved stock utilisation was also a factor in stock reductions with for example the use of Class 442 units on most fast Portsmouth services in addition to maintaining their duties on the Bournemouth line. The old stock on the Waterloo & City line ran its last services on May 29 when the line closed for re-equipping to allow operation by the new Class 482 units.

At this time BR seemed a little reluctant to sell locomotives for scrap with a large collection at Tinsley, for example, while at March no fewer than 14 Peaks still rested among the weeds where they had arrived at least two years earlier.

Services
The Robin Hood line opened for passengers on April 27 running from Nottingham as far as Newstead, the intention being to run through to Worksop – a target that was still a few years away from fruition. Even the initial short line proved popular and the service frequency had to be doubled to cope with the number of passengers which were predicted to total 33,000 in the first year.

Greatly improved services from Worcester to Paddington, nominally worked by the new Class 166 units started with the summer timetable and brought immediate rewards with passenger numbers up by 26% leading BR to say that it might consider further service enhancements.

The line to Manchester Airport was brought into use on May 16. When Swindon built DMUs took over Trans Pennine services back in the 1960s some units carried headboards proclaiming Trans Pennine Express. The title fell into disuse but was officially revived although apparently not carried from May.

The BR annual report for 1992/3 was published at the end of June. An operating surplus of £13.4m in reality became a loss of £164m after interest charges and redundancy payments had been taken into account. Despite the loss £1,384m was invested in the system, up 19% on the previous year. Of note was the fact that no passenger was killed in a train accident, this being a marked improvement on figures seen at times in the previous decade. That said, the definition was carefully drawn as there were still a considerable number of fatalities on railway property of both the public and employees. Illustrating the safety tightrope being walked was a derailment at Maidstone East involving a freight that at times was said to convey nuclear waste. The line was blocked for three days but the driver was arrested for being over the drinking and driving alcohol limit, was dismissed and awaited trial at the year end. Although the lines were cleared in three days the complete clear up operation took over a month and rebuilding until the year end.

Signs of progress in the building of the South Yorkshire Supertram system were evident with the line from Meadowhall to the city centre the first section to open. Extensions to Halfway and Middlewood were scheduled for completion by 1995.

New on the former Southern region were the two-car Class 466 units, used both on lightly loaded lines but more so to make up formations from 4 to 6 and 8 to ten cars. 466008 was found at Bromley North in March. Colour-Rail.com

Another line to enjoy new stock was the Waterloo and City system where the Southern Railway era stock was well past its sell by date. The new Class 482 units were derived from the London Transport stock being delivered at the time and in would pass into the ownership of that body. 482503 was seen at Bank in July 1993. Colour-Rail.com

Britain's Railways in the 1990s

Thirteen of the trams running in Manchester had received names. It was claimed that anyone who was prepared to pay enough to the operator could have a tram adorned with the name of their choice as it was deemed to be advertising.

An interesting co-operation between the network and a heritage line saw the running of a landcruise train which originated at Kings Cross and got to Darlington via Haltwistle hauled by a Class 47. This was then joined by a 37 and working in top and tail mode the train then ran to Levisham on the North Yorkshire Moors Railway where it stabled overnight before going to Whitby the next morning and thence to Kings Cross.

A major change to mail train services saw a number of historical trains withdrawn. From the summer there were 24 scheduled trains although all were balancing duties so effectively there were 12 services although a few, such as the Carlisle-Peterborough train, did not follow the same route on the outward and return journeys. However there were signs of BR losing its grip on the moving of post and parcels with Royal Mail's Mailsort traffic being lost to road competition. This led to a reduction in the number of trains and also the need to add/remove carriages enroute with at least two station pilot duties being lost as a consequence. Despite this a new 13-year contract was signed for the carriage of mail by rail along with a commitment to purchase 16 UK-built mail trains, eventually arriving as Class 325 EMUs.

Another long running saga that seems no nearer to a conclusion today than it did then was a proposal to re-open the Stratford to Honeybourne line.

The early 1990s saw another period of economic woes with a continual trimming of freight services and facilities. In the South Wales coalfield area every month seemed to bring about 'the last train' from one of the once numerous dispatch points and the commentary generally was that freight traffic was at the lowest levels anyone could remember. Even the still quite buoyant aggregates industry produced fewer workings as train lengths had been increased with the arrival of classes 59 and 60. The economic situation also brought about substantial passenger service reductions, particularly in the Southern commuter belt. Even the Isle of Wight felt the pinch with just one train per hour being provided in the winter timetable.

Motive power on Paddington to Worcester services in respect of power classification had almost mirrored that used on the Waterloo-Exeter route, but services were now to be worked by air conditioned Turbo units of Class 166 and 166209 was heading for Worcester when seen at Charlbury on August 14. D Pye/Colour-Rail.com

Manchester Airport station opened for business in 1993. Long-distance services were supposed to be worked by Class 158s but the shuttle service from Piccadilly was initial entrusted to displaced 305s. The station environs still have the 'just built' look in this view taken on December 6. Colour-Rail.com

Britain's Railways in the 1990s

1993

When 47288 derailed and overturned at Maidstone East it caused considerable damage to the infrastructure but also raised concerns about nuclear waste being moved through the area although none was carried on that particular service. The loco awaits rescue on September 6. D Ovenden/Colour-Rail.com

A new service in Scotland saw the opening for passenger use of the Rutherglen-Langloan freight line. Thirty two trains per day were provided from Glasgow Central to Whifflet with rebuilt or new stations at Carmyle, Mount Vernon, Ballieston, Bargeddie and Kirkwood.

The Merseyrail electrification project to Hooton and Chester went live from October 4, giving a 15-minute service frequency at Hooton and 30 minutes at Chester. Some Class 508 units for the service had been stored at Llandudno Junction.

Operations

Unsurprisingly the winter weather caused havoc, although mainly confined to Scotland in January. A very heavy snow fall followed by heavy rain and a thaw saw extensive flooding particularly north of Dundee and Perth with predictions that some lines might be closed for at least a month.

A new livery took to the rails to denote locos working for BR Telecommunications. This was applied to 20128/31 being two shades of grey with a large green BRT logo.

The Network South East paint scheme continued to be applied to units but those operating on the Southern Central Division started to receive Network South Central branding.

An InterCity promotional train which ran from June 26 to July 1 took a Class 91 and Mk IV stock including a driving van trailer (DVT) all over the West Coast mainline. 91001 was in charge and was seen at Glasgow, Euston, Manchester, Liverpool and Wolverhampton during its perambulations.

As from the start of the Summer timetable Birmingham New Street saw a lot of activity using Class 308 EMUs as the full Cross City service through to Redditch commenced using the type although some DMU duties remained. A daily appearance of a Class 165 was noted the type being used on the 17.10 to Hereford.

With Merseyrail gearing up for its extension to Chester, some 'new' shunting locos were required for depot and permanent way (PW) duties and 73001/2/5 arrived at Chester for evaluation for the work.

Coal imports and their associated trains started to feature more often with one such flow being from Teesside to Longannet and Cockenzie power stations, these frequently employing Inverness based 37s, these making what had been rare visits to the Teesside area.

Running-in turns for ex works locomotives were once a common sight with many actually being a slow run on a scheduled passenger service or double heading an express attached to the loco rostered for the duty but the separation of the workshops from the day to day activities of the railway had seen the setting up of test trains composed of passenger stock demoted to departmental use. Even these were now becoming a rarity but at least Doncaster works retained its test train that usually ran northwards to Tyne Yard and of course any loco repaired at Doncaster might appear and noted on consecutive days in March were 20131 and 86634.

One of the more fanciful namings, on April 21 was for EMU 320322 rather than a locomotive. The chosen name *Festive Glasgow Orchid* related to the 14th World Orchid Show which was being held in Glasgow. It is not thought the name remained attached for long.

A job to keep various workshops busy for a few months was the fitting of secondary door locks on slam door stock for Intercity which still had some 1900 such carriages in its fleet. Crewe and Derby were the main sites for the work but Devonport, Stratford and Kilmarnock were also involved.

Another cruise by the ship *Canberra* was made on June 12 and once again a boat train was provided at the Southampton Western Dock. A passenger train also visited the Eastern Dock on 19th, being the first rail movement there for over twelve months. It was a railtour topped and tailed by 47463 and 37375. In fact things were looking up with a regular freight conveying Rover cars using the Western docks.

Provision of a station pilot, once almost obligatory at any sizeable station, was becoming increasingly rare. The latest to go was at Edinburgh Waverley with any further shunting requirements to be carried out by the train engine.

The fate of the workshops at Doncaster, Eastleigh, Glasgow and Wolverton plus the Level 5 depots at Chart Leacon and Ilford hung in the balance as they were announced as being offered for sale as one entity.

When HST sets got into trouble they would normally be rescued by a class 37 or 47 but a rare occurrence saw electric 90025 so employed on September 23 working from York to Doncaster before being substituted by the more regular 47.

Intense diagramming of many DMUs and EMUs saw 'miles run' accumulate rapidly and October 26 saw 156405 become the first unit of its class to reach the million miles mark, this being achieved in not much over five years.

Heritage

The Kent & East Sussex Railway announced ambitious plans for 1993 having seen a sharp

The Merseyrail electric system saw a large expansion of its network when through-working to Chester began. 508132 approaches its terminal station on August 10. R Siviter/Colour-Rail.com

Britain's Railways in the 1990s

Station pilots had been a feature of Britain's railways for the best part of 150 years but the need for their services in the 1990s was disappearing rapidly. Edinburgh Waverley lost its Class 08 pilot in 1993, said to be due to the reduction in mail traffic. Interestingly however this view suggests that most duties were performed on behalf of the Intercity sector as 08570 carried their livery at Waverley in June 1991. Colour-Rail.com

With the changing railway scene the role of the traditional workshops had diminished almost to nothing whilst once off the beaten track 'carriage sheds' became Level 5 depots, making them responsible for much heavy maintenance. One such was Ilford, photographed during an open day in 1989. D Pye/Colour-Rail

growth in passenger numbers despite poor economic data. Service frequency was to be increased although that would employ smaller engines like the resident A1X tanks on two coach formations with daily running from Late May until October 1 rather than just in July and August.

The East Kent Light Railway had its Light Railway Order signed on August 31. BR agreed to sell them the trackbed for £24,738, this then inflating to £32,000 with VAT and legal fees. Fundraising was stepped up as a matter of urgency.

Another Kent line, the Sittingbourne & Kemsley celebrated 25 years of heritage operation but unfortunately a deterioration in the concrete structure of the elevated section of the line saw services suspended there with a temporary terminus station constructed at Milton Halt. The cost of the viaduct repairs were estimated at £300,000.

The end appeared to be in sight for one of the first preservation sites when H P Bulmer announced that the land used for the railway centre at its Hereford plant was required for expansion although no date for closure was suggested but the end was in fact swift coming at the end of May.

April 13 saw what may have been a 'one off' mainline happening when all three restored Stanier Pacifics: 6201, 46203 and 46229 were in steam together at Llandudno Junction. The three of them worked various stages of the Ynys Mons railtour that day.

Scotland gained a new preservation centre with the opening of a site for the Ayrshire Railway Preservation Group who were based at Dunaskin ironworks and also Minnervy colliery, the two connected by a three mile running line.

In March the Swanage Railway was able to offer a true London and South Western Railway (LSWR) experience with trains worked by M7 30053, T9 120 and Bulleid Pacifics: 34072 and 34105. The final service of the day saw the Pacifics double heading, thought to be a preservation first. Plans were for an extension through Corfe to a new terminus at Norden and late in the year work started to level the sight. Two thirds of the required £90,000 had been raised.

The Isle of man railway provided, and still does a train

44

Britain's Railways in the 1990s

1993

The future of the Sittingbourne and Kemsley Railway was brought into focus when the elevated section of the line was discovered to be atop a then crumbling concrete structure in Sittingbourne. It was no longer safe for use by passenger services pending expensive repairs. In this view, predating the problem, passengers were still allowed to travel standing up in open wagons. Colour-Rail.com

service that stopped just a very few minutes from the island's airport, thus offering the discerning traveller the opportunity to commence their travels from the island by commuting to the airport on a one hundred year old steam train, an experience almost certainly not available anywhere else in the world.

Steam returned to the full route from Exeter to Waterloo on September 5 in the shape of 34027 *Taw Valley* which started its journey from St Davids and was banked to Central by 50007/50. S15 828 was another performer on Southern metals seven days later when it stood in for the booked 777 when it worked from Eastleigh to Waterloo via Andover. A third train ran on 26th on the same route this time with 828 and 34027 double heading for part of the journey. Brighton and Dover also saw their first steam workings.

Some heritage lines set out to always portray a particular period or operating railway, but engine loans and gala days can sometimes completely change the offering. On August 7 the Severn Valley Railway managed to be almost completely BR Western region by using 4566, 7325, 7714, 7819 and 75069 and the East Lancashire Railway turned out 2857, 3822, 6998, 35005 and 53809 on the 13th.

A main line excursion that did not go to plan ran on October 16 involved 44871 working from Fort William. As icy rails were encountered the train slipped to a stand. Bound for Edinburgh Waverley it arrived at 03.00. Another steam tour was planned for later in the day and some who were participating in both stayed on the train as it journeyed to Bo'ness for servicing. The second train, with 60532, also had adhesion problems requiring assistance from a Class 56.

Several years after closure there was still railway activity on the site of Swindon Works where a leased building was in use for restoration and repair with five locos on site, 4612, 5521, 7812/21 and 80072. The pattern shop, weighbridge and turntable still existed but a large warehouse was under construction on the site of C Shop. ∎

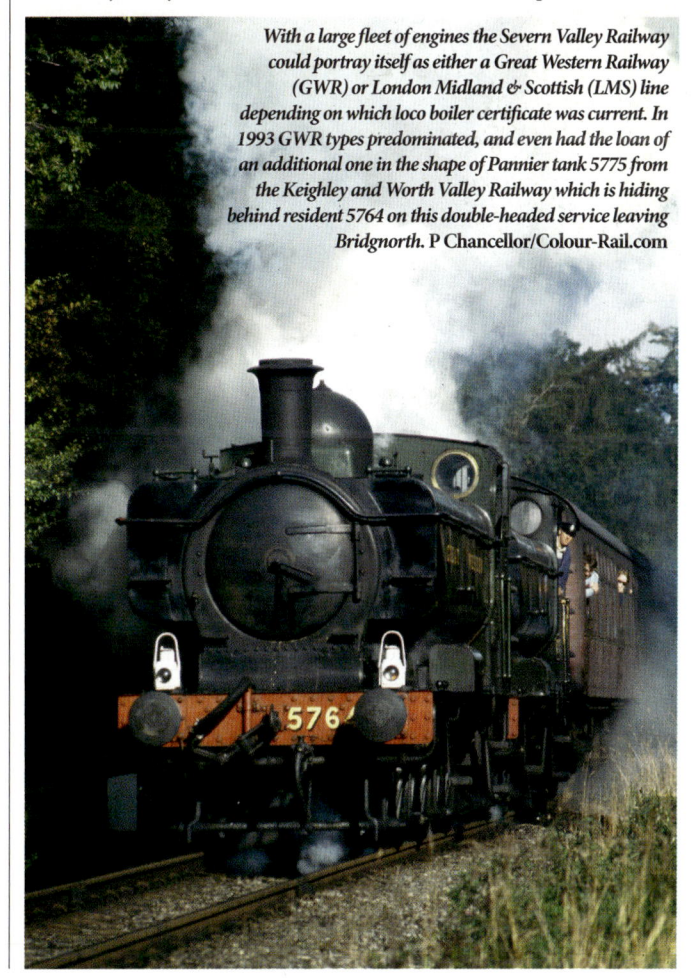

Some heritage lines were able to recreate scenes from their past by running locomotives appropriate to the area. One such was the Swanage Railway which had National Collection T9 120 on loan in 1993. P Chancellor/Colour-Rail.com

With a large fleet of engines the Severn Valley Railway could portray itself as either a Great Western Railway (GWR) or London Midland & Scottish (LMS) line depending on which loco boiler certificate was current. In 1993 GWR types predominated, and even had the loan of an additional one in the shape of Pannier tank 5775 from the Keighley and Worth Valley Railway which is hiding behind resident 5764 on this double-headed service leaving Bridgnorth. P Chancellor/Colour-Rail.com

Britain's Railways in the 1990s

1994

CHANNEL TUNNEL LINK OPENS

Some looked forward to 1994 with much optimism – others could predict only gloom and destruction. These were the two sides of the rail privatisation debate, somewhat akin to the more recent Brexit decision. Indeed the year was to see the practicalities of a privatised railway, for which all the restructuring of the previous two to three years had been preparing for. Railtrack had opened for business but its impact on daily operations would not be seen until April. One of the first new proposals that it would have to consider was that of the electrification of the line from Edinburgh to Glasgow where a study by Scotrail, the Passenger Transport Executive (PTE) and councils had concluded that there was just a viable case for a scheme costing £25m for the route via Falkirk High. More adventurous proposals costed at £50m for 100mph running and a train every 15 minutes could not be justified.

In other organisational matters a Rail Regulator had been appointed to represent the interests of passengers and rule on intercompany industry disputes. The government set out more 'expectations' including ticket inter-availability and thus common pricing which was to be part of franchise agreements. Railrover tickets appeared to be under threat but were guaranteed until the year end.

One of the downsides for enthusiasts was that the supply of stock change information looked set to cease from the end of March. Some operators might be prepared to supply it, but others would certainly claim 'commercial sensitivity'. The latter became apparent, as information such as official dates of withdrawal ceased to be known in many cases, a movement to the scrap yard becoming the only signal of impending demise.

The names of the rolling stock leasing companies emerged as Eversholt, Porterbrook and Angel. Perhaps this was the business to be in as unlike almost every other organisation involved with the early days of privatisation these survived. When the allocation of rolling stock between the three was announced it also emerged that RES would own a substantial fleet with all excursion stock, parcels/mail vehicles and the Royal Train moving to them. Eversholt took the lion's share of the rest of the hauled stock with Porterbrook just having the West Coast Mk III carriages. High-speed train (HST) stock followed the power car split with Porterbrook and Angel splitting it, while for diesel multiple units (DMUs) Porterbrook had mostly second generation and diesel electric multiple unit (DEMU) stock. Angel had the rest with the EMUs being split fairly equally among the three.

It appeared to be anticipated that there would be much surplus equipment being put up for sale by British Rail (BR) and the Government suggested that those interested in running their own freight services should contact BR to purchase some of the items such as wagons and locos. The timetable for freight privatisation envisaged a sell-off to the private sector in 1995.

It might have been expected that under the new regime assets would be tightly controlled with the correct freight company locos supplied from the appropriate pool for each duty. However, an early observation at Hull suggested that the reverse was the case where nine freight duties in early April should all have been worked by locos from the same pool and

46   *Britain's Railways in the 1990s*

1994

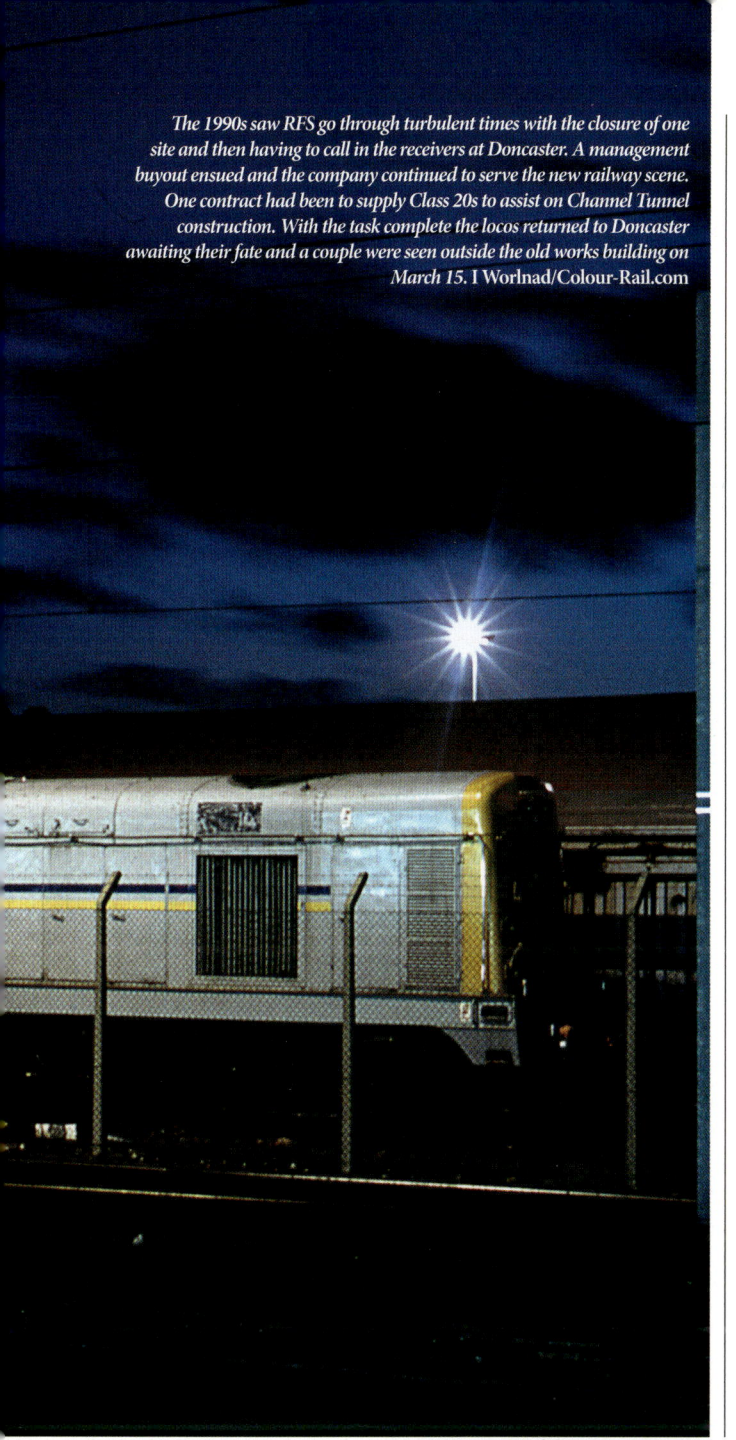

The 1990s saw RFS go through turbulent times with the closure of one site and then having to call in the receivers at Doncaster. A management buyout ensued and the company continued to serve the new railway scene. One contract had been to supply Class 20s to assist on Channel Tunnel construction. With the task complete the locos returned to Doncaster awaiting their fate and a couple were seen outside the old works building on March 15. I Worlnad/Colour-Rail.com

more work on the books and complete closure appeared likely.

After many months of wrangling a 'final decision' was announced for the route of the Channel Tunnel high-speed rail line. Kings Cross had frequently been proposed as the terminus but the report came down in favour of using St Pancras. Links to both the East and West Coast routes were proposed to enable the running of through trains. A lot of the line within the capital was to be underground and would go via Stratford and Rainham and crossing the Thames in a tunnel from Thurrock Marshes coming up in Kent at Swanscombe Marshes. Beyond Gravesend it would follow the M2 and M20 motorways for much of the rest of the route. Ebbsfleet was suggested as the most likely interchange station but the economic case for one at Stratford had not yet been made.

The opening of the tunnel had an undesired side effect for those working at Harwich on the Zebrugge ferry. Redundancy loomed with the intention to route all railfreight through the tunnel. Wembley was to be used as the consolidating yard with trains being diesel worked to Dollands Moor until at least the end of 1994 when Class 92 haulage would be phased in. With no sign of an about-turn on the provision of regional passenger services a new depot was being constructed at Longsight.

Invitations to tender were issued to build the new high-speed link. The £1.3bn debt for construction was to be split between Railtrack and BR. Railtrack could recover its share via track access charges but the £900m share attributed to BR would have to be recovered via higher fares for all rail users.

Wrongly wired

Cable theft had long been a problem for the railways, usually causing a high-degree of disruption. But thieves needed to become a little more discerning in their target as technology moved on and fibre optic cables were deployed. So, when 300 yards of cable was 'lifted' from Barnetby in March it caused predictable travel chaos but the thieves took away cable with a zero scrap value.

The opening of the first phase of the Sheffield Supertram project took place on March 21 being open from Fitzallan Square to Meadowhall. Trams were running on an eight minute frequency with a travel time of at worst 50% of that by the competing buses. The livery at the time was 'overall grey'.

With the demise of BR some lines were again seen as under threat of closure and the dormant Cambrian Lines Action Group was reformed to protect that route. On the other side of the coin Gwynedd County Council and Regional Railways were to spend £100,000 on promoting the line but Railtrack were soon on the case of realising their acquired assets by offering the car park at Porthmadoc for sale.

An early impact of privatisation was seen on April 1 when the buffet at Faversham station closed, said to be due to the property board demanding a 100% rent increase. The scale of track access charges was seen in the South Yorkshire Passenger Transport Executive (PTE) area, these being quoted at £10m for the year compared to a total operating cost of £6m in the previous year. A 20% fare rise in 1993 was followed by 10% in 1994 with another large increase expected for the following year.

The recently refurbished Waterloo & City line became part of London Underground from April 1.

shed actually produced locos from six pools and four sheds.

British Rail demonstrated that it could still move quickly when required as following a washout at a bridge west of Welshpool the route through to Aberystwyth looked likely to be breached for several weeks. Within a week temporary halts had been constructed either side of the bridge with passengers transferring between trains by walking over the bridge.

Meanwhile, privatisation was not boding well with the need to call in the receivers at RFS Doncaster. A rescue buyout was organised by five managers late in 1994. In 1993 the catering company providing refreshments on the Salisbury-Exeter line also ceased trading leaving a number of hungry travellers as finding a replacement always took time. Another company in trouble was Hunslet of Leeds, who having completed the order for Class 323s had no

With the new terminus for Channel Tunnel services at London St Pancras it was clear the station appearance would alter dramatically and so it would soon be farewell to this view inside the train shed. D Pye/Colour-Rail.com

Britain's Railways in the 1990s

47

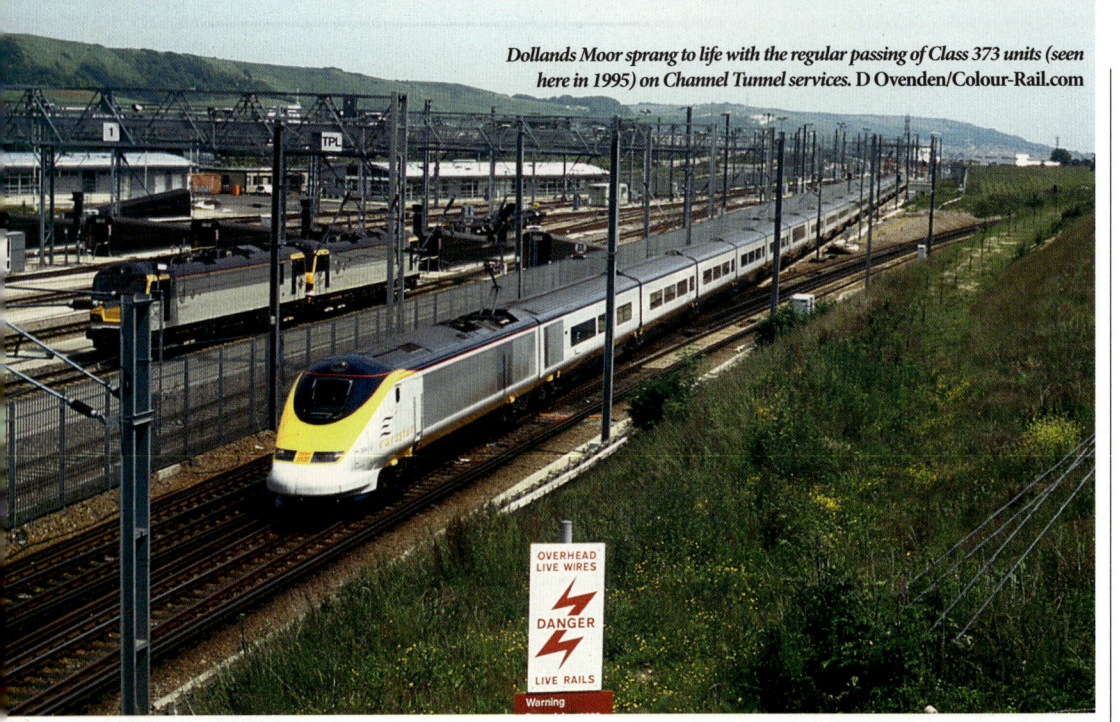

Dollands Moor sprang to life with the regular passing of Class 373 units (seen here in 1995) on Channel Tunnel services. D Ovenden/Colour-Rail.com

The new scene must have been a boon to the signage industry as each of the new operating areas and companies sought to 'state their ownership' by indulging in a programme of rebranding stations and other facilities across the country.

The first sign of the new order in the freight businesses was the emergence of 37713 and 56039 in a black and orange paint scheme branded for Load Haul, this being the company designated as North East. However, many locos just carried Load Haul branding on their BR grey. The other two names were announced as Transrail, which would always retain BR grey and Mainline (the South East company) who would in due course paint some engines in a rich dark blue with probably the first to appear being 58050 in early October. Another new livery was seen for Waterman Railways on 47710, this being described as London and North Western Railway (LNWR) black. This was possibly the first 'spot hire' loco in the new era and it was noted working a postal service from Newcastle on July 11.

On the safety front, the first death of a passenger for at least two years occurred on June 25 when 303046, working from Wemyss Bay to Glasgow hit an obstruction on the line. It was derailed and then hit a bridge abutment.

Modern technology possibly averted at least one death when a Class 37, 37113, rolled away from its stabling point at one of the platforms into the path of an incoming HST at Edinburgh on August 13.

Signalling staff could monitor the movement of the 37, although not divert it, and were able to contact the driver of the HST. He was able to slow his train and move to a position of relative safety within his cab.

Tragically, technology could not prevent the deaths of five people when two DEMUs collided head on near Cowden on October 15.

After a long period that had seen only occasional and mostly unofficial strikes on the railway, signal staff in the National Union of Rail Maritime and Transport Workers (RMT) walked out on

Here 56077 passes through Barnetby in September 1991. The rural station was home to some major items of semaphore signalling that were added to in 1994. Colour-Rail.com

1994

for days in June and early July. Very few trains operated on the strike days. Further days of action followed at around weekly intervals until the dispute was finally settled in late September although more trains were operated during each subsequent strike.

Crossrail seemed to have rapidly disappeared from the agenda with the privatisation process occupying much management time. Some 78% of the top London companies expressed support for the project.

The Level 5 maintenance depots came under the British Rail Maintenance Ltd (BRML) umbrella with each to become a self-contained limited company in readiness to be sold to the private sector, not as one group as seemed probable previously.

Stock Changes

The first of the National Power 59s, 59201 arrived in the country in February and became available for training in April but the balance of the order for six did not arrive until 1995.

The notification of transfers of the whole locomotive stock to new pools to reflect the 'ownership' under the coming privatisation was made on March 31. One consequence was the demise of the Class 50s with the three remaining 50007/33/50 being withdrawn although use in the previous few months had been almost entirely on specials. It also showed the vast number of withdrawn engines awaiting disposal totalling nearly 300 most of which were split between the three new freight operators.

The new EMUs for the Southern region were not put to traffic in any specific order and were still entering traffic at the start of the year with, for example, 465161-3 and 466011/7/40 being nominal January additions. That said, true to BR reporting, while put to stock, some of the units were still at the constructing works.

Trams returned to the streets of Sheffield carrying a very underwhelming grey livery as seen here. P Hughes/Colour-Rail

With Railtrack established, it was not long before it sought to dispose of assets. 150145 is pictured at Portmadoc, the site of one of the first disposals with the sale of part of the car park. Colour-Rail.com

By mid-year nearly all had been delivered and the first of Class 365 were imminent, these being the 25Kv version of the design for use on services from Kings Cross. The end of the reign of the Class 308s on the Birmingham Cross City line appeared to be imminent with the start of entry into service of the 323s with first use noted on February 7 but mixed stock workings persisted for many months.

One of the first casualties of the year was the Class 309 EMU. The whole class had been expected to be withdrawn but the 309/3 variant units passed to Regional Railways for further use. Others were the electric train heating ex-locomotives or ETHELs – the scourge of many photographers who when taking photos of mainline steam in the winter months were almost certain to see one of the machines appear behind the tender.

The end came in December for the 2 HAP design of two car EMUs on the Southern. Originally numbered in the 6XXX range when new in the early '60s the final units in service carried 43XX numbers.

92001/2 were moved to Prague in February to be evaluated on a test track there and also a test station where the effect of various climates could be evaluated. 92003 was to be sent to France for the testing of the in-cab signalling system. Thirty-seven of the fleet were intend to haul freight with the other nine put to overnight sleeper services. Work on another servicing depot, this time at Polmadie, got underway. There were plans for departures to both Brussels and Paris each day from Glasgow with a journey time of around eight hours. 92001-10 were shown as 'to stock' at the end of July but as well as 92001-3 abroad 92006 was also in France, 92005 was at Brush and 92010 in store at Kineton leaving just 92004/7-9 on BR. Twelve Class 37s were under conversion to become 37601-12 being intended for powering the night trains which were not running under the wires.

Both the naming and subsequent removals continued at pace during the year. Names occasionally appeared on multiple units but were virtually unknown on hauled stock but this was about to change, at least as far as the DVTs were concerned with West Coast 82101 being one of the first being noted carrying *Wembley Depot Quality Approved*.

March saw the completion of two Scotrail projects with £2m having been spent on the renovation of Wemyss Bay station and £3m to build new maintenance facilities for both DMUs and EMUs at Corkerhill shed.

There still appeared to be an interest in heritage where on the Southern three 'preserved' 4 EPB units soldiered on with 5176 joining the group, well restored in traditional BR blue livery.

50   *Britain's Railways in the 1990s*

1994

Launch of the three new freight companies saw a mini boom for suppliers of orange paint when Loadhaul used the colour as part of its new livery. The first Class 56 in the scheme was 56039, ex-works at Doncaster in July 10. P Hughes/Colour-Rail

The Glasgow Underground system, better known as the Clockwork Orange, was refurbished in 1980 with new stock. This led to a marked growth in traffic and a number of two-car sets had just been strengthend to three cars with the arrival of the then new centre cars.

The use of Class 323s expanded when the first of the ones allocated to Regional Railways Northwest entered service on Manchester Piccadilly-Airport services.

Services

Services started from Birmingham Snow Hill to Marylebone, apparently on an hourly frequency on Saturdays. Northwards from Birmingham regular EMU services commenced to Liverpool.

Over the years there had been a number of accidents at Stourbridge Town station with DMUs failing to stop at the bottom of the steep descent from Stourbridge Junction and ending up in the bus station. From April 24 this became less likely as a new station was opened, this being a few coach lengths away for the bus station which had also been rebuilt.

A service reopening project was partially completed on May 30 when the first part of the Ivanhoe line between Leicester and Loughborough calling at Syston, Sileby and Barrow on Soar became available for passenger use. A number of other 'single' new stations were opened around the network during the year such as Ivybridge on July 15, along with the rebuilt station at Gunnislake. The latter's new site did not have enough room for large buses to turn and they grounded on the road camber. Perhaps a little consultation with the operator at the design stage would have helped. No such problems were reported at a new station at Wallyford, east of Edinburgh.

Car ownership in the Lothian region had increased by 50% in ten years and traffic congestion was becoming a major issue. More new stations were proposed in the area along with an idea that the Waverley-Galashiels line be re-instated, services having ceased in 1969, at a suggested cost of £30m.

One of the first freight contracts planned for Channel Tunnel use was signed with Transfessa which would move car components for Ford from Valencia to its UK factories with a train running every day. Three hundred new wagons were required and these would include gauge change capability as the Spanish Railways still employed five-foot gauge track.

A service which for many years attracted enthusiast interest disappeared from the timetable from May 28, this being the Clapham Junction Kensington Olympia service known as the Kenny Belle. Having latterly been worked by an EMU the replacing service was a DMU from Clapham to Willesden Junction. No service was offered at weekends.

The new livery chosen by Waterman Railways, all over black, looked good when fresh and clean but unfortunately it did not last for long. 47710 was the first loco to carry it along with a new design of nameplate proclaiming that it belonged to the 'Heritage' class. D Pye/Colour-Rail.com

Britain's Railways in the 1990s

New paint schemes abounded in 1994 and the choice by National Power for its Class 59s certainly caught the eye. 59201 appears to be an exhibit at Rugeley power station on July 10. D Pye/Colour-Rail.com

Scheduled locomotive hauled trains from Swansea ceased on May 28 the last being the Swansea-York and return services. Rescheduled for HST working the route was amended to run via Bristol.

Another new service from South Wales to Waterloo routed around the west side of London. Worked by HSTs this brought the type to Waterloo for the first time. Another Channel Tunnel feeder service employed Class 158s from Manchester, routed via Salisbury but not calling there. It became the first daily service since the Devon Belle to omit the stop.

Operations

The Channel Tunnel opened on May 6 when Queen Elizabeth II and other dignitaries took the sub-terranean journey from Waterloo to Coquelles for the official ceremony. Despite all of the enthusiasm on the day, regular public services were not expected to start before October. The following day a steam special behind 70000 but in the guise of 70014 *Iron Duke*, arrived at Folkestone with the passengers then being taken to the tunnel site. On the 8th a Class 319 EMU was in use from Ashford running trips directly into the tunnel. The first through-freights from Willesden ran on June 27. Regular passenger services started on November 14 with two trains to Paris and one to Brussels daily and it was not long before reports of failures and delays appeared in the railway press – these happening before the start of the scheduled services. With rescue locomotives based at the North Pole depot in West London it could take quite some time to reach a failed set in deepest Kent.

Under the new regime, if a passenger sector required extra stock or locomotives for occasions like summer service extras, it had to be hired in. For Summer Saturday Norwich-Lowestoft trains Anglia agreed to hire a Stratford based Cl. 37 from the Infrastructure pool, although what was actually supplied could often differ, such as Res 47575 being employed on August 19.

Class 37s were regularly deployed on North Wales coast workings, continuing into the winter service, and they were

The Hunslet built Class 323s spent a long time stored around the system awaiting acceptance into service. Some were kept at MoD Kineton including 323204, seen on March 12. Colour-Rail.com

52   *Britain's Railways in the 1990s*

1994

Having given the best part of 30 years of service in East Anglia some Class 309 units avoided the scrap yard when made redundant in 1994 by moving to Regional Railways Northwest. Prior to the move 309626 was serving commuters at Chelmsford on January 22. Colour-Rail.com

used on the Bristol-Weymouth line for Summer Saturdays.

It is often said that an ill-wind blows nobody any good and that adage proved true following a derailment at Hungerford on September 5 involving Yeoman hopper wagons. During investigations into the cause, the wagon type was withdrawn from use, accounting for about half the Yeoman fleet. Replacement alternatives were obtained from several sources including departmental stock, giving local freight wagon spotters an enjoyable few weeks.

Most signalling schemes saw the replacement of semaphore signals by colour lights but at Barnetby, where the down slow lines were being re-instated new semaphore signalling was installed.

The unprecedented failure of a cable at the Edinburgh signalling centre looked set to cause major and ongoing delays to services at Waverley. Many speed restrictions were introduced and some services were curtailed due to problems accessing the line from Edinburgh to Glasgow via Carstairs. Other services were diverted around the suburban lines to reach Waverley from the East.

Class 158 duties had generally settled into fixed patterns with a new service employing the class from Manchester Airport to Glasgow Central. Meanwhile, some locomotive-hauled trains had returned to the Inverness-Edinburgh service.

Locos were also set to return to some Inverness-Kyle duties.

The availability of Class 91 locos on the East Coast route had seen the almost continual use of hired in class 90s as cover, usually two or three at a time from 90021-4. Unusually, March saw some of the Res liveried examples appear with all of 90017-9 being seen but even more surprising was the use of one of the West Coast passenger pool 90004.

Use of unfitted freight wagons, noted in 1993 as being confined to trains for Alcan in northeast England, came to an end on January 21 when ten converted PGA wagons, previously used for cement replaced the unfitted PAO type.

Great lengths were taken to keep passengers happy and on the move when a bridge required replacement at Carlisle between Upperby and Citadel station which required a complete line block for just over two days. Regional Railways built a temporary platform at Upperby and provided toilets, a refreshment caravan and an information cabin. Through services continued to run via the goods lines with passengers for Carlisle being bused to and from Penrith.

A pair of Class 73s ventured to the North Wales coast on March 12 working what was described as a Merrymaker excursion. The locos concerned 73002/6 were from those allocated to Merseyrail for stock shunting and permanent way (P Way) work and while 73002 ▶

The name ETHEL became the scourge of those taking winter pictures of steam hauled mainline trains as they were frequently coupled behind the engine to heat the train. Despite their blue and grey 'camouflage' they stood out in almost every picture. The demise of 97250-2 came in 1994. The last member of the class is seen at Marylebone. Colour-Rail.com

Britain's Railways in the 1990s

Another class to reach the end of the line was the 2 HAP EMU, later known as Class 414. Originally numbered in the 6XXX series they later moved to become 43XX and 4317 is pictured at Staines West. Colour-Rail.com

retained large logo blue livery 73006 was in Merseyrail yellow.

With the reduction of locomotives that could affect a rescue of a failed passenger train plus the advent of sectorisation where it became necessary to get the authorisation of the 'owner' before a loco could be used for such a mission, Thunderbird locos started to be specifically allocated for such duties and were stabled at strategic points on the system by some operators. Those in use on the East Coast route became the responsibility of Res with 47520, 47671/3/5 being the nominated engines.

Enthusiasts over the years learnt they should always beware of the validity of official information supplied on interests such as withdrawals and allocations. An example of this could be seen in May at Tinsley where 08919, officially transferred to Crewe in January was in store and 08581, which should have gone to Doncaster in March, remained operational Tinsley. It was also observed that the vast marshalling yards were almost unused with just five lines in operational use and another five contained condemned stock.

At an Exeter rail fare on May 1 and 2 there were a number of special trains and engine workings including runs behind 20118/31, triple-headed 37s 37796/9 and 37898, 59004 and BR Standard tanks 80079/80. Steam engines and heritage diesels were displayed alongside more than 20 mainline locos which included 90128/33 along with representatives from most active classes.

Another of the 'benefits' of the new system was that an army of accountants was now employed in attributing delay costs which had to be paid by the operator who caused the delay. An interesting debate might have been had when an HST failed on the Lickey incline. 60032 was sent to rescue it but the HST drawgear was damaged during the attempt. Very long delays ensued trapping several trains with one not reaching New Street until 02.30. Taxi fares and hotel bills alone were estimated at £5500.

Despite Class 37 by now being almost the largest single class on the network, the type were surprisingly rare in some areas, particularly in Kent and what was thought to be the first use ever of one on a freight on the South Eastern division mainline was recorded on August 5 when 37892 when it rescued a failed service at Ashford.

The problems posed by new technology were demonstrated when 321901 failed at Stoke summit on a two track section of the East Coast mainline, the unit being enroute to Doncaster after overhaul at Wolverton. The only motive power on that part of the East Coast line that could couple to the 321 to move it was a Class 317 EMU, the process of finding one, getting it to site and subsequent removal took in excess of four hours during which single line working had to be implemented causing long service delays.

One of the more recently constructed depots on the network, Cambois, closed on September 19 with its duties being transferred to Tyne Yard.

Depot allocations increasingly seemed to be becoming less relevant, particularly for shunting locos with some of those allocated to Allerton being located at Dover, Southampton, Wembley and Dagenham among others.

Train services were disrupted by flooding around Glasgow from

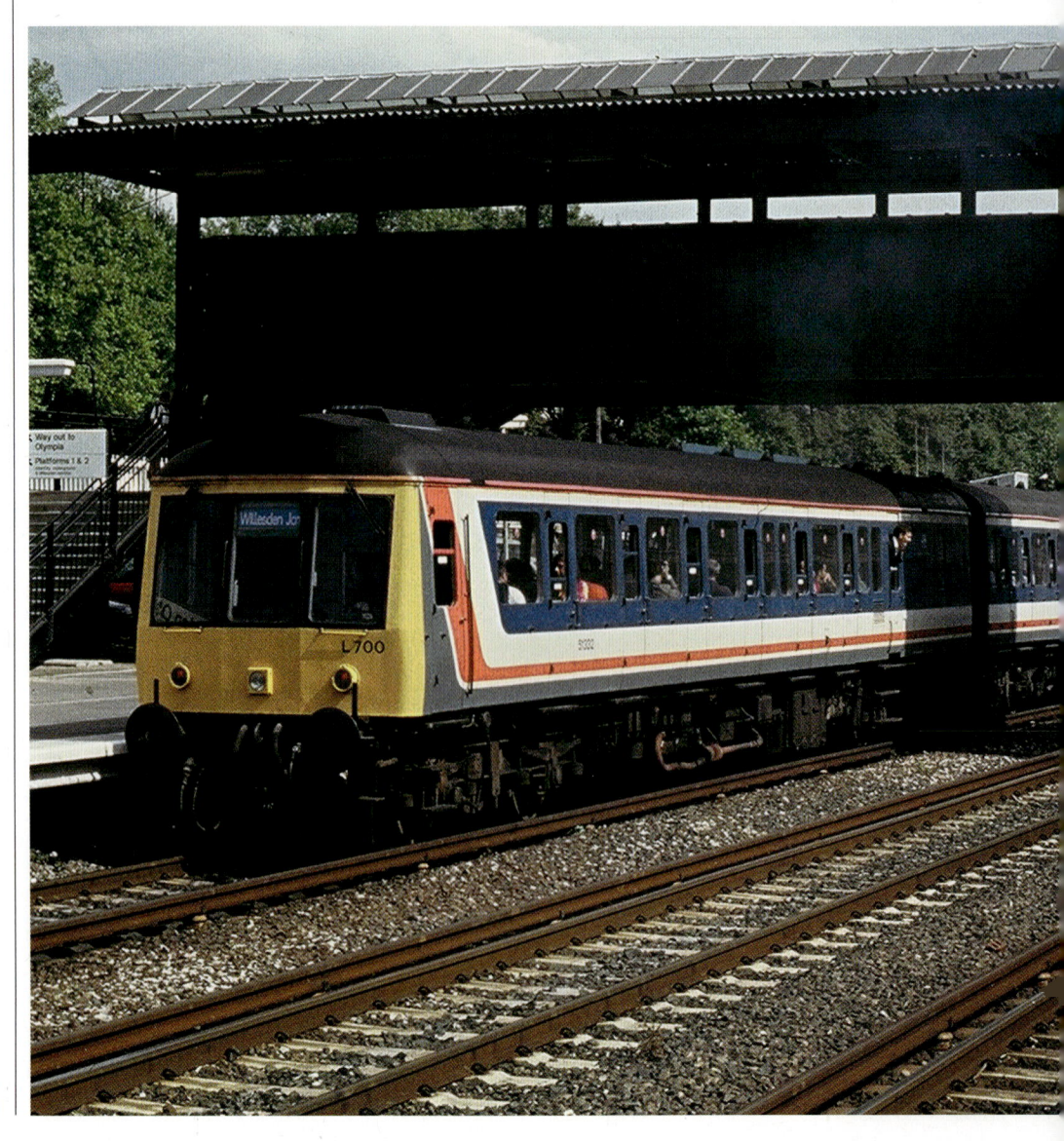

1994

An interesting excursion in April took a pair of Class 73s for a run along the North Wales coast where they were photographed on a dull day leaving Rhyl. Colour-Rail.com

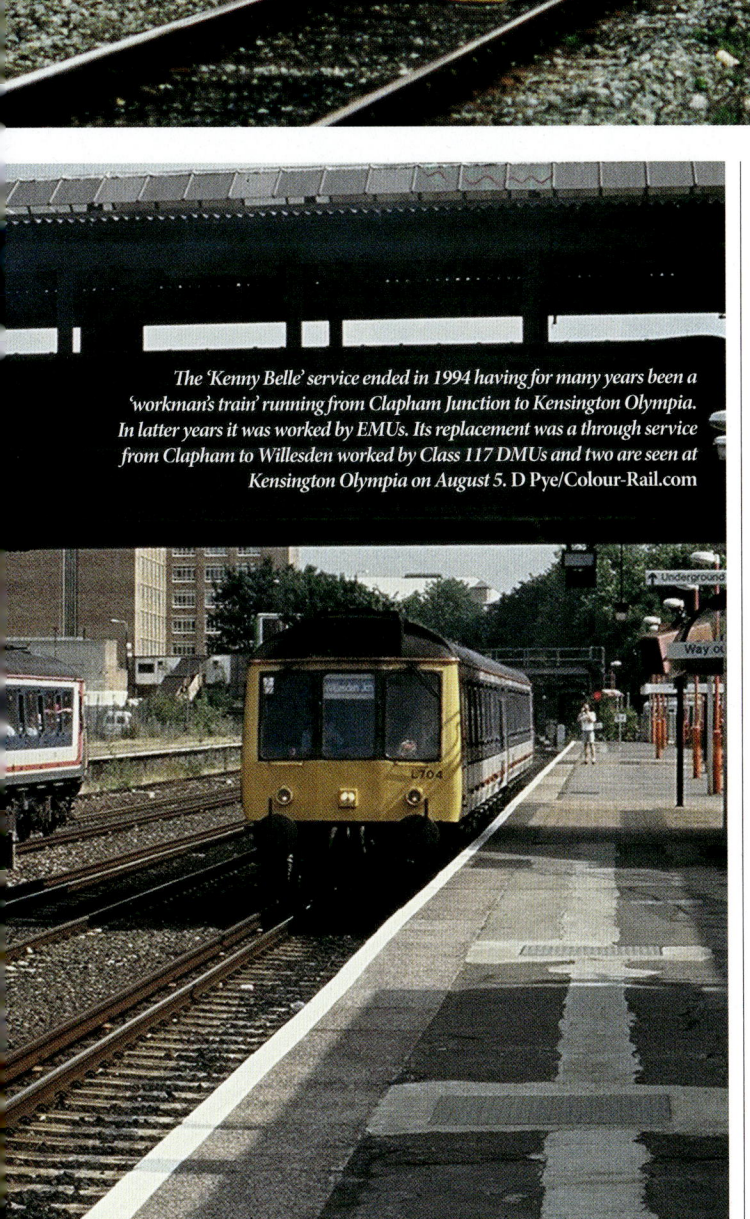

The 'Kenny Belle' service ended in 1994 having for many years been a 'workman's train' running from Clapham Junction to Kensington Olympia. In latter years it was worked by EMUs. Its replacement was a through service from Clapham to Willesden worked by Class 117 DMUs and two are seen at Kensington Olympia on August 5. D Pye/Colour-Rail.com

December 9 until at least the 15th. A local press picture showed an EMU at Glasgow Low Level submerged up to window level. There was damage to tunnels on the Argyle line and trains there not restored by the year end.

Heritage

A locomotive of historical interest returned to the country from Austria in January – the former Gas Turbine 18000 – which was seen at Tinsley. However it lacked nearly all of its internal equipment.

Another extension to the Glouces-Warks railway came into use for the new season, this being the 1.5 miles from Gretton Meadow to Stanley Pontlarge making the round journey up to ten miles.

At the Midland Railway Centre attention was turned to the restoration of Caprotti fitted Standard 5MT 73129 and an appeal was made for funds totalling £5,000.

The well-known Welsh narrow gauge lines had been operational for many years and another name from the past looked likely to join them before long, that being the Corris Railway. Some track laying had already taken place from Corris to Maespoeth but the local council now granted permission for an extension through to Pantperthog which would make the line two miles long.

The spiritual home of the Hull Locomotive Preservation Group, the former Dairycoates depot in the city, was scheduled for demolition. Although the two engines most associated with the group, Stanier 5MT 5305 and the NRM's 777 spent most of their time away from the area, there was still stock at Hull which needed a new home including Crab 42859 which remained untouched since its rescue from BR.

The South Yorkshire Railway based in Sheffield had built up an extensive collection of diesel locomotives, many being ex BR shunters and included the first Class 14 D9500. Its latest acquisition came in the shape of the first BR built 350hp shunter D3000 from the Brighton Railway Museum. This had been rescued in 1987 after 14 years of use by the National Coal Board.

The demise of British Rail was marked by running steam specials on the North Wales Coast line on April 1 and 3, employing five engines: 828, 4498, 5029, 46203 and 71000 – one from each of the 'Big Four' plus 71000 representing the BR era.

Some residents of Kingscote were probably 'not happy' when the Bluebell Railway started services to the station on April 23. The council had imposed a number of restrictions when granting planning permission including one that tickets from Kingscote could only be sold to those arriving by bus.

Plans for a railway museum based in the former Pullman Works at Brighton were abandoned due to site access problems. A number of locos intended for the scheme never actually reached Brighton with 3845 34046 35009/11 being

Britain's Railways in the 1990s 55

Is this perhaps the furthest any West Coast electric travelled away from the wires? 90133 was one of the locos displayed in Riverside Yard at Exeter during an event on May 1 and 2. Colour-Rail.com

stored at Hove goods yard for at least the last five years. Another site to close, but due to insolvency, was Chatterley Whitfield mining museum which was home to North Staffordshire 0-6-2T No. 2, which moved to Cheddleton. Many other ex-industrial engines remained on-site awaiting new owners.

4-4-0 *Glen Douglas* escaped from the confines of Glasgow Transport Museum with the approval of a seven year loan agreement with the Scottish Railway Preservation Society. It was hoped to restore the engine to working condition while at Bo'ness.

Heritage lines seemed to be taking a keen interest in acquiring redundant DMU cars at this time with for example Wales Railway Centre, Caerphilly Railway Centre, Chasewater and Mangapps all receiving such in the summer. However some cars that had been rescued were being sent for scrap. This appeared to be associated with the use of asbestos during the construction of the vehicles. With the regulations tightening, heritage lines could often not afford to restore cars containing the hazardous mineral and the railways could no longer dispose of them to heritage lines without getting it removed.

Quite rare for the time was the return to working order of heritage diesels and one to note was Class 44 D8 *Penyghent* at Peak Rail which had not been operational since moving into preservation in 1980.

An unusual double naming ceremony occurred on November 30 when a jumbo jet and Standard 2-6-0 76079 from the Llangollen railway both took the name *Castell Dinas Bran* at Heathrow airport.

On completing its contract, the former Western Region gas turbine loco 18000 moved to Switzerland but returned to the UK in 1994 and was temporarily stored at Tinsley. It is seen here while resident on the continent in 1987. Colour-Rail.com

56 *Britain's Railways in the 1990s*

1994

The Hull locomotive Preservation Group was given notice to quit its long-term home at Dairycotes and its operational engines were rehoused at the Great Central Railway. 42859, pictured, was not so lucky becoming embroiled in ownership disputes in subsequent years. This view dated from December 22 1990. Colour-Rail.com

Strange that the engine had to be moved to London rather than the jumbo dropping in at Llangollen.

The Barrow Hill Engine Shed Society were carrying out some tidying up at the former shed pending news on a grant application to save the building. Unfortunately, in the meantime thieves helped themselves to some of the track in the yard.

A catastrophic incident occurred when 60532 *Blue Peter* slipped just south of Durham station on October 1. The slipping was severe due to the crew being unable to shut the regulator and wheel speeds reached an estimated 140ph before the motion and cylinders suffered terminal damage. Some of the remaining parts of the motion had to be dismantled before the train could be moved. The incident removed 60532 from duties for many months.

An important milestone in mainline steam seen on October 29 was the first steam special from Kings Cross which saw 60009 *Union of South Africa* make an early morning departure from the Capital enroute to Peterborough on a very dank autumn day. ■

Bluebell Railway trains arrived at Kingscote in 1994 for an envisaged short-term use of the terminus, but things don't always go to plan. Much restoration, including commissioning the signalling system, remained to be completed. The new signal box at Kingscote is seen on the 'night shift'.
P Chancellor/Colour-Rail.com

Dringhouses yard, on the west side of the line south of York station, had been a major freight train destination for many years. But changing traffic patterns made it redundant with the land put up for sale in 1995. Back in June 1979 it was still relatively busy as can be seen here as 55015 passes. G Parry Collection/Colour-Rail.com

1995

TAKEOVERS AND BUYOUTS TIME

In the new era any organisation could be contracted to carry out locomotive overhauls and with that in mind 56107 was sent to Brush at Loughborough for a 'pilot' overhaul to allow them to quote for further work. The ownership of Rail Express Services (Res) passed to Wisconsin Central of America and BRT to Racall Electronics.

Asset disposals by Railtrack and the BR property board seemed to be gathering pace with the former large Dringhouses goods yard at York and the coal yard at Scarborough being sold. A new rail connected Royal Mail hub at Low Fell opened in March. A small 'tidying up' of operational areas saw the Ashford-Hastings line and the Coastaway service to Chichester and beyond come under the control of South Central, making South Eastern an all-electric area.

A new light rail scheme had an unspecified amount of money set aside by the Government to build the Croydon Tramlink, proposed to run to Wimbledon, Beckenham, Elmers End and New Addington. It was to have both street running and use some railway trackbed. Also authorised was a start on the Midlands Metro, which required significant funding from local sources. The proposal was for a 12-mile line from Wolverhampton to Snow Hill via West Bromwich and Bilston.

A permanent way slowing at Wallyford due to subsidence caused considerable delays and would cost £800,000 to fix. The problem was due to a mine shaft that was not on any maps but repairs had been necessary in 1885 after the original line had been laid across the unmarked shaft in 1846. Clearly the miners who were Monks in the 13th century were to blame for this problem through failure to lodge maps with the appropriate authorities.

Issues concerning safety involving Railtrack were already emerging. Lineside litter and maintenance, a perceived unsafe roof at Scarborough station and the apparent condition of the Forth bridge, where repainting work had stopped, were early signs of problems that would surface in years to come.

Another preparatory move for privatisation saw Freightliner established as a separate business unit being split out of Railfreight Distribution and their branding appeared on 47157 and 47270.

With new train orders drying up the ABB works at York that had built thousands of carriages over the years looked set to follow Hunslet in Leeds by closing its doors. However, compared with the situation a couple of years earlier the fortunes of ABB Crewe seemed improved with around 30 locos present including two HST cars and even one EMU, 314208. At ABB Derby some maintenance work

Traditionally the Forth rail bridge was repainted on a continuous basis but concerns were being raised about its current condition and with apparently not a painter to be seen in 1995. From a distance however it still looked good as 47633 headed across. R Siviter/Colour-Rail.com

Britain's Railways in the 1990s

1995

on both diesel multiple unit (DMU) and electric multiple unit (EMU) vehicles was under way along with the construction of stock for London Underground. The Rail Maintenance sites at Glasgow and Wolverton also seemed to have a reasonable workload. However it would seem that changes might be on the way as it was announced that the latter two had been sold to Railcare – a consortium of Babcock International and Siemens. Other sales were Ashford, Doncaster and Ilford to ABB Customer Support Limited. Eastleigh had a management buyout under the name Wessex Traincare.

As predicted, tax payers' money was invested in 'claiming ownership' of stations by rebranding. Under the new regime Railtrack had ownership of a number of the major stations across the network – an example was Edinburgh Waverley. It repainted the station in green and grey and replaced the InterCity and Scotrail-branded station name boards for those with Railtrack green flashes. The only evidence that Scotrail worked from the station was one large illuminated 'Welcome' sign. This soon became 'Welcome to Waverley Station– a Railtrack Independent Station', but clearly that message did not meet with approval. It was changed to 'Railtrack welcomes you to Edinburgh Waverley Station'. Another sign on the south side even incorporated the BR Arrow symbol. A similar desire to spend public money was seen at Leeds.

A development that was to have far-reaching effects saw 321308 become the first train to carry an all-over advert. Future developments saw the 'wrap' technology used to apply new liveries as well as advertising.

The three leasing companies were sold at the end of the year. Angel was bought by a consortium of organisations including a Japanese-based investment bank with the other two going to management buyouts with additional financial backing.

The end of the year appeared to bring the first announcements of a franchising agreement, one covering the very much self-contained Fenchurch Street to Southend was a management buy-out. The franchise plan was for the Class 302 units then in use to be replaced by 317s, the latter made redundant on West Anglia services by the delivery of Class 365s. On a much larger scale Stagecoach was the successful bidder for the South Western division of the former Southern Region.

Stock Changes

With the industry engrossed in privatisation measures both deliveries of new stock and disposal of nominally redundant locos and rolling stock almost ground to a halt. The only locomotives arriving were class 92s and 59202-6 which were put to stock in late August - being the balance of the order for National Power. It would seem that the former were to be the last mainline railway locomotives built in Britain as the next new engines were the Class 66s. 47488 47701/3/5/9/10/2 were sold to Waterman Railways.

Despite only being in service for a couple of years some Class 60s were losing their BR-allocated names and receiving commercial replacements, such as 60059, formerly *Samuel Plimsoll* became *Swinden Dalesman* complete with a large Tilcon badge plate.

With Class 92 locos having different owners only those belonging to Railfreight Distribution carried the double arrow while SNCF-owned examples carried its insignia. Those for EPS at least initially did not carry any evidence of ownership. Two of the four Mirrlees engine high-speed train (HST) cars 43167/70 were the first to be fitted to receive VP185 engines at ABB Crewe but the actual fitting took place at Laira, 43167 having been out of use for three years. They were joined later in the year by 43168/9 making the Mirrlees variant extinct. Some power cars allocated to Neville Hill were also designated to receive VP185 engines with 43047 being the first noted. Despite the change in the way things were managed some items continued to move at a snail's pace. HST power cars 43071 and 43180, both 1994 accident victims, were still awaiting a contract for repair at Crewe at the end of 1995. The Great Western train operating company (TOC) agreed an interior refurbishment programme for its HST cars leased from Angel.

The last Southern EMU to carry rail blue and grey livery 2 EPB 6259 was withdrawn in January. The 2 HAP class, apparently made extinct in December 1994, reappeared in traffic on January 16 due to ongoing unit shortages due to the continuing delay in getting Class 465s in to service. The 465 situation had improved by March and the HAPs along with all CAP and EPB units except 5001 and 5176 were condemned. The first 4 CEP units were withdrawn in June.

The first of the Royal Mail-owned EMUs 325001 broke cover in March and was on test at Warrington on March 20.

The external appearance of the Class 142 sprinters was changing with the start of a programme to replace the Leyland National four leaf bus doors with two-leaf sets. Although only having been in traffic for a few years

Crewe Works was a shadow of its former self by the 1990s. A visit in 1996 found few locomotives under repair but 08911 was identifiable in August that year and the number of locomotives being repaired had risen from recent numbers. T Owen/Colour-Rail.com

Enter the vinyl wrap. A lot of plastic film had been used to wrap the whole of unit 321308 but the system did allow liveries to be transformed literally overnight and it would see a rapid adoption by the industry. The unit was seen at Liverpool Street on August 19. D Pye/Colour-Rail.com

Britain's Railways in the 1990s

Things did not move quickly when more than one organisation was involved. HST car 43180 sustained accident damage and spent nearly two years out of use. With the operator, the workshop, lessor and more involved it was never going to be simple but its revival was fast approaching in Crewe works on August 17 1996. R Hunter/Colour-Rail.com

In the past any depot might have been asked to supply Royal Train locos although the Western region appeared to provide most in more recent years from the Intercity pool of Class 47s. One of the favourites was 47834, seen here with the royal stock near Stoke Prior on a snowy March 3. R Siviter/Colour-Rail.com

evaluation of various fabrics for a refurbishment of Class 156 units were under evaluation in 156450.

The Royal Train had an outing on March 3. Under privatisation such duties were the responsibility of Res but the traditionally used locomotives were part of the Intercity fleet two of which 47834/5 were duly supplied. In future only one company would become responsible for the locos, rolling stock and crew this being addressed by designating two Res locomotives for Royal train duty with the two from the Intercity fleet becoming 47798/9 with Res. Intercity livery was replaced with the Royal 'maroon' and the locos were renamed *Prince William* and *Prince Harry* respectively.

In a move that would be replicated in due course on the national network, London Transport concluded a contract with GEC Alsthom which would see that company be responsible for the ongoing maintenance of stock that it supplied. Meanwhile the last train of '93' stock was handed over on March 13 and the final run of 62 stock ran on February 17.

An event that attracted little attention and even less information was the trial of a Parry People mover at Barking in June.

In what in subsequent months would turn out to be the setting up of DRS, British Nuclear Fuels were reported as having purchased 20084, 20113/75 with these moving to Brush, Loughborough for repair. In fact seven Class 20s were involved with five to be outshopped as 20301-5 in the new DRS blue livery. with the other two being used for spares donation. A further three engines were being stored on behalf of BNFL at the Midland Railway centre. Trials with 20301 were carried out at the Great Central Railway.

The Southern was still using some diesel electric multiple units (DEMUs) and seemed to be constantly reforming and renumbering sets as the numbers required reduced. Some class 207 units had a coach added to their formations, these coming from 4 CEP EMUs. However, one was coach 71634 that in turn had originally been from hauled stock as 4059. This gave it the distinction of being the only carriage used in hauled, EMU and DEMU formations with its history dating back to the mid-1950s. The units were used on Ashford-Brighton services.

The Special Trains fleet, comprising 141 carriages plus a number in store transferred to the ownership of Waterman Railways Charterail from April 1. The electrification scheme from Leeds and Bradford to Skipton saw power on (except in the Leeds station area) throughout from April 24 with crew training beginning using Class 308s. Though most passenger electric workings ran from early July, the first services were noted on May 26. As a result, some Class 141 units became redundant and were returned to the lessor. They were physically located at Doncaster initially.

The engine involved in a runaway incident at Edinburgh Waverley in 1994, 37113, was cut up at the Freightliner depot at Portobello with work beginning in April but not completed until mid-August, almost exactly a year after the event. Reflecting the disconnect between the real world and industry records, the latter recorded the engine as withdrawn in September, some weeks after the remains were disposed of.

The end was in sight for Bristol Bath Road depot at the end of May

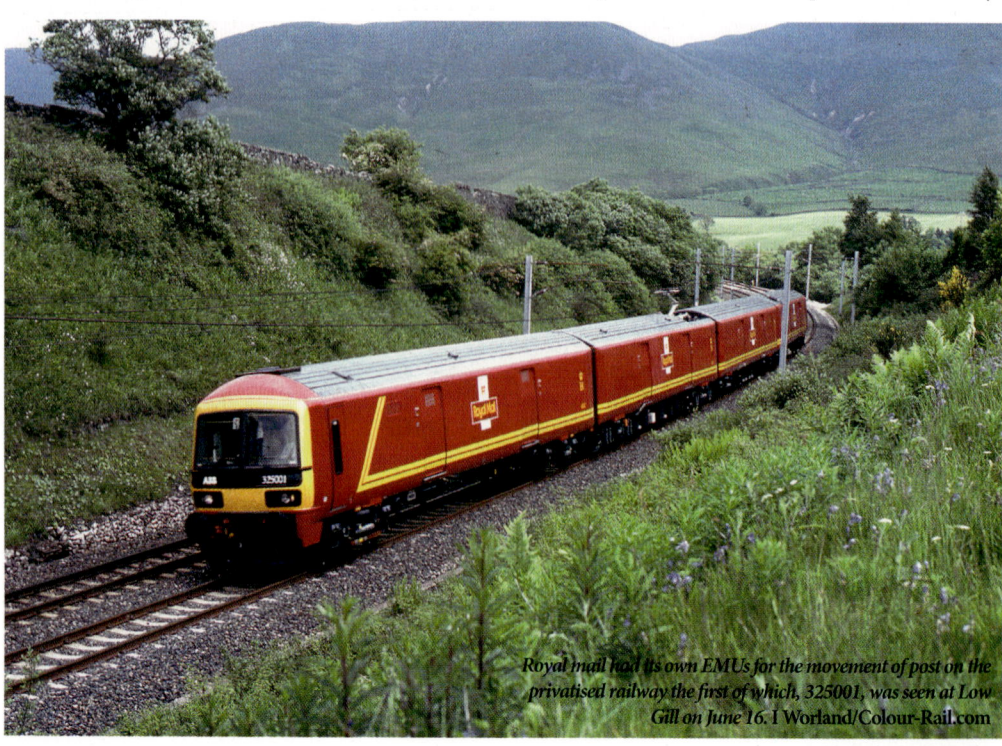

Royal mail had its own EMUs for the movement of post on the privatised railway the first of which, 325001, was seen at Low Gill on June 16. I Worland/Colour-Rail.com

60   *Britain's Railways in the 1990s*

1995

Class 47s were the normal power for royal duties but there were some lines where their axle load was deemed too great. Presumably that is why, when the train needed to traverse the Cambrian lines, substitute power in the shape of DRS's recently acquired Class 20s 20301/2 were provided and were caught on film near Machynlleth on May 31 1996. It is doubtful if DRS had anticipated such a duty when it bought the 20s. T Owen/Colour-Rail.com

when the whole of its allocation, which consisted only of InterCity Class 47/8s was transferred to Crewe. Complete closure came on July 24 with any required loco maintenance and stabling moving to a new depot at Barton Hill.

Keeping the accountants happy led to some 4 VEPs operated by South Eastern being renumbered. All of the incumbent units were leased from Angel trains but eight new arrivals belonged to Porterbrook. So that the costs could be correctly attributed, the new comers were renumbered from the 34XX series to the 38XX series to aid easy identification.

In December a large number of locomotives, particularly Cl 31 were transferred to 'HQ' pools which generally indicated being out of traffic. However, none were recorded as withdrawn and throughout the whole of the year notifications of withdrawal were probably at the lowest ever recorded, the trend being for locos to be retained in store 'just in case' a new traffic flow or increased demand surfaced.

Services

There had been several instances of 'trying something different' in providing passenger services since the creation of the new train operating organisations. One example was a Birmingham-Paddington service via Kidderminster but this was withdrawn in May after just two years of operation, removing Class 166 units from the Birmingham-Worcester line.

The South Yorkshire tram system continued its phased opening reaching Shalesmore on February 19, Halfway on March 27 and Herdings Park on April 2. The final stage of the Sheffield Supertram system opened on October 21. The Manchester trams were proving popular and it became necessary to investigate ways of increasing capacity, this being attempted by reseating tram 1017 to carry fewer seated but to create more standing room. Another place looking at a light rail system was on the south coast to run from Southampton to Portsmouth.

No stock was ordered when approval was given for the electrification of the line from Leeds and Bradford to Skipton. Consequently, when services started in 1995 improvisation was the name of the game. West Yorkshire liveried 308136 is seen approaching Shipley on August 15. Colour-Rail.com

Britain's Railways in the 1990s

Bristol Bath Road shed had attracted enthusiasts at the station to the platform end to see what was on shed ever since it was built. The twists of fate ensured that it ended its days with just a handful of Intercity class 47s to look after and when they moved to Crewe closure was inevitable Strangely in this view, whilst 47569 and others are in view, Intercity examples appear to be absent. Colour-Rail.com

Specially modified class 37s were required to work with Channel Tunnel passenger stock and 37601-12 were provided for the job, but with developments not going to plan a number seemed to be surplus and employed elsewhere. Quite how 37611 ended up parked at Stafford, however, we shall probably never know. Colour-Rail.com

A new destination reachable from Waterloo became available from July 3 when HST worked trains to and from Edinburgh were introduced.

Services to and from Manchester Airport had settled into a regular six arrivals per hour with short turnaround times and on time departures being essential to prevent delays. Generally loadings were good with the longer distance services being the fullest.

Although it was initially difficult to gauge freight activity through the Channel Tunnel, on March 17 92022/3 were thought to have made the first run of the class through to France in service. Eight Class 47s were at Dollands Moor and on 22nd 37601 made the first visit of one of the dedicated EPS locos. Passenger services were scheduled at up to six per day from April. A survey in August suggested that up to 30 freights per day were working through but at that time all were diesel hauled from/to the tunnel but the loaned SNCF electrics returned home.

The summer timetable change saw a proposed retrenchment of Scottish sleeper services with just two trains, one terminating at Inverness and the other Aberdeen with the service to Fort William no longer operating. However, the Scottish High Court had ruled that, because the correct closure procedures had not been followed, Fort William should remained served, the estimated cost being £2.5m over 12 months. Also deleted were all Motorail services from Euston. So, the Fort William sleeper was running but there were no class 37 trained drivers at that depot and crews were sent by taxi from Glasgow at a cost of £140 per day. In September the Rail Regulator ruled that the service must continue to be provided for at least seven years. Attempts to revive freight by rail on the Far North lines saw trial loads of steel, coal and pipes, all worked by Transrail motive power.

A new station at Charlton Hundred, between Grays and Ockenden opened on May 26 and Smethwick Galton Bridge did so two days earlier. The next stage of the Robin Hood line opened to Mansfield Woodhouse on November 20 thus removing Mansfield from the list of large towns with no railway station. Services commenced on the Jewelry Line from Birmingham Snow Hill to Smethwick on September 24. These ran through from Leamington and Stratford to Stourbridge Junction.

The Maglev train system at Birmingham Airport, opened in 1984 closed in June needing expensive repairs. It was not expected to reopen. The Docklands Light Railway opened its branch to Beckton on December 16.

Crew training needs combined with a reshuffle of units brought about the introduction of a loco-hauled diagram on Rhymney-Cardiff trains with Waterman's 47488 being the regular power initially.

Signs of some business enterprise began to show through such as a proposal by Network South Central for a through service from Brighton-Rugby worked by Class 319s with the intention it should start in May 1996.

Operations

The year got off to a bad start with a passenger death resulting from a collision between two Class 156 units on the Settle & Carlisle line at Kirkby Stephen when one was derailed by a landslip, the circumstances sounding much like the recent accident at Carmont. The train that was derailed was returning north having found the line blocked by flooding and then hit the landslip, subsequently being run into by the next southbound service. In what turned out to be a frightening prelude to the horrendous crash of 1999 an HST set and a Class 165 collided at Royal Oak on November 10 but no deaths occurred on this occasion.

Loco duties continued to evolve as traffic requirements changed. At one time Class 58 was employed almost entirely on coal duties but with the ongoing reduction of UK mined coal they were now appearing over a much wider

The Robin Hood line reached as far as Mansfield Woodhouse in 1995 when the new station was opened there. J C Haydon/Colour-Rail.com

No doubt deemed to be a good investment at the outset, the Maglev cars connecting Birmingham Airport to Birmingham International station ran for only 11 years. One of the cars is in action here in 1985, soon after opening. Colour-Rail.com

area and hauling other traffic including oil on occasions.

The flooded Argyle line, damaged in December appeared to be unlikely to reopen until at least May and perhaps later. To aid pumping the water out of the tunnels a hole in the tunnel lining from street level had to be made. In the end repairs were not completed until September and then the re-opened line was flooded once more on October 24, this time the rain being accompanied by storm force winds, bringing down many trees and power lines.

Free of the constraints of a national livery policy, some of the business units turned out locos in 'alternative' paint schemes while others harked back to the sixties with one example being 47517 which reverted (almost) to its 1966 state in two tone green as D1102. Only the shape of the yellow panel and the various light fittings and brake pipework betraying that it was 1995.

ScotRail seemed intent on promoting itself as an independent organisation because as well as getting its logo on all of its multiple units in large lettering it was having the double arrow symbols removed. Also going were branding such as 'Super Sprinter'.

The changing scene was illustrated by Knottingley depot which, when opened, was the preserve of Class 47s, these then being ousted by 56s. Now these had all gone to be replaced by Class 60s.

A new diagram starting in January for a Western region HST took a set to the HST desert of Liverpool from Euston arriving in the city late on Saturday evenings and leaving again at 10.45 on Sunday morning.

Tytherington Quarry and its associated branch from Yate rejoined the network on February 9 with the first train of aggregates headed by the Mainline liveried 58050.

MC Metals, who had cut up many BR carriages at Margam started to receive many Southern EMUs, thus giving spotters along the route the unusual opportunity to underline a considerable number of such trains, just in the nick of time.

Class 37 duties on passenger services over the North & West route continued but for the first time in over five years a Class 47 worked one of the duties when 47739 was turned out on February 12.

Class 33s 33109/16 ventured to Scotland in early May where they were used on the line between Cumnock and Annan in conjunction with the filming of a film starring Tom Cruise. They were seen stabled at Ayr on May 5.

The at the time sole Class 59/2 59201 was normally to be found operating in Yorkshire but made a surprise appearance at Peterborough on April 22 en route to March to collect a single wagon.

Triple-headed Class 37 duties returned to the network following adhesion problems working Aberthaw-Cwmbargoed MGR duties which loaded to 27 wagons. If only two 37s were available then the load had to be reduced to 18 wagons.

A railtour brought three Class 31s to Kent, a type rarely seen in the county, with them even working to Folkestone Harbour, which was thought to be as first for the class, this happening on May 13.

Promotional activities for services were usually left to the train operating companies but the Penistone Line Partnership provided a once-per-month boost for travellers on the evening service to and from Sheffield with a folk group and a real ale bar being arranged to enliven the journey.

Class 58s took over Avon Binliner duties from June bringing regular visits by the class to the area for the first time.

Birmingham temporarily became a Mecca for EMU enthusiasts with duties for classes 308, 309, 310, 312 and 323 with the 312s finding favour on duties to Liverpool.

The Glastonbury pop festival, which had seen plenty of extra rail services over the years, continued to grow in popularity. Local shuttle services were DMU-worked but extra HSTs, along with loco-hauled trains using both 37s and 47s, were provided.

The breakage of a single insulator brought major problems for Channel Tunnel passengers on the 07.13 Paris-Waterloo on April 12. Having been brought to a standstill not far into its UK travels it could go no further and had to be rescued and shunted by 47299 back to Dollands Moor – which took until after midday. Passengers were then disembarked via the doors in one end carriage undergoing customs checks at that point before having to walk the length of the sidings with their luggage to waiting coaches with arrival in the capital after 16.00.

Another example of questionable decision-making in the new arrangements involved the Class 153 units for the Central Wales line which started their day at Swansea. Originally stabled at Landore, with the split of business units Landore did not do any work for Regional Railways, which led to empty coach stock (ECS) running to and from Carmarthen for night stabling.

With trials of 365501 apparently complete, further units of the batch were seen being tested between York and Darlington in September.

Heritage
A new restoration site was opened at Thingley Junction at the old MoD sidings where Polish 0-6-0T 4015 and Battle of Britain 34053 were among the first residents.

Birmingham briefly became a mecca for EMU spotters with up to five types operating on any one day. Brought in from eastern England were a few Class 312s and 312727 was noted at Wolverhampton. J L Champion/Colour-Rail.com

Britain's Railways in the 1990s

A new Arrival on the mainline list was Standard 4MT 75014 which worked a test train on March 3 and piloted 70000 southbound over the S&C on 31 on a special marking the last run of the Special Trains unit which passed to Pete Waterman the next day.

'Steam ignorance' struck once more on January 25 as King 6024 was 'brewing up' at Temple Meads; as the fire service was called out by a member of the public to put out 'the fire'.

Illustrating that landslips were not a phenomenon confined to the national network, the Bluebell Railway had to suspend services between Horsted Keynes and Kingscote following such an event on February 16.

The project to restore Barrow Hill Roundhouse looked likely to go ahead with a decision by Chesterfield Council to spend £350,000 on repairs. It was also anticipated that there would be a visitor centre and training facilities.

Since its announcement in the early 1990s the project to build an A1 pacific had gathered enough momentum for a start to be made on planning its construction under the name of the A1 Locomotive Society, with the old carriage shed at Darlington being selected as a base. The chosen identity to be carried was 60163 *Tornado*.

At Peak Rail, steam reached Rowsley for the first time since 1968 on January 29 when 0-6-0ST *Warrington* worked there to rescue D2128 which had failed on a works train.

A Pannier tank that had never been the subject of a real preservation attempt, 9629 moved to the Pontypool and Blaenavon Railway in February. Since 1986 it had been displayed outside the Marriott Hotel in Cardiff. The challenge for those restoring it was that it did not have a boiler which had been fitted to 3650 at Didcot.

A number of mainline steam trips in Southern England were cancelled in May due to an increase in fire risk and even some that did run caused a problem such as one of the rare outings by the SVR 2-6-0 7325 which lit a number of fires between Hereford and Worcester. The ban later spread to throughout BR and indeed in August even to the Severn Valley Railway.

Starting an association that lasts today, 35028 *Clan Line* worked to Canterbury and Dover at the head of the Venice-Simplon Orient Express (VSOE) Pullman stock with the train named as the Golden Arrow.

As noted in the Network news, the Midland Railway Centre hosted some engines on behalf of BNFL. This was one of the first instances of Heritage lines providing facilities on behalf of network operators, these being a cheaper and/or more practical alternative than having to deal with Railtrack and pay their charges.

The East Kent Railway started services from Sherherdswell to Eythorne on June 24 these being formed of a 2-car Class 107 DMU. Services also got under way at the Nottingham Heritage Centre.

A new preservation group the Aln Valley Railway Preservation Society was formed to promote the re-opening of the Almouth-Alnwick line, closed in 1968 and targeted for revival in 2000. The projected cost was £4m. Meanwhile the Avon Valley Railway extended operations by 0.5 miles to Field Grove Farm but no station was provided.

Work at the Mangapps Farm Railway included starting work on a new station towards Burnham on Crouch, the buildings previously having been at Laxfield.

The plan to set up the Mid Norfolk Railway between Dereham and Wymondham received a boost when Breckland Council offered a grant of £25,000 and an interest free loan of £100K. However that still left a funding gap of £275,000.

Part-way to fruition was the recreation of a broad gauge layout at the GW Trust site at Didcot. The transfer shed, used to move goods from broad to standard gauge wagons was complete with track being laid and construction of a replica broad gauge engine *Firefly* was deemed to be 50% complete. ■

1995 saw a close association develop between the operators of the Venice Simpleon Orient Express and those who looked after 35028 Clan Line. *Later it was often seen heading the train complete with a Golden Arrow headboard. On this occasion it was at Sevington. Colour-Rail.com*

BR Standard 4MT 75014 joined the mainline stud briefly and occasionally double-headed with Britannia 70000. When not out on the network it found employment on the North Yorkshire Moors Railway and is seen near Green End. P Chancellor/Colour-Rail.com

An ambitious project to recreate a section of broad gauge railway along with a transfer shed and appropriate locomotive was under way at Didcot. The finished article is seen here with 'Firefly' on the broad gauge and Beattie well tank 30585 on the standard in May 2007. P Chancellor/Colour-Rail.com

Britain's Railways in the 1990s

MAGAZINE SPECIALS

ESSENTIAL READING FROM KEY PUBLISHING

MODELLING BRITISH RAILWAYS
Modelling Railfreight

£8.99 inc FREE P&P*

BRITAIN'S RAILWAYS IN THE 1980'S

£8.99 inc FREE P&P*

ROLLING STOCK REVIEW 2022/2023
The 212-page title contains almost 2,000 updates compared to the 2021 edition.

£8.99 inc FREE P&P*

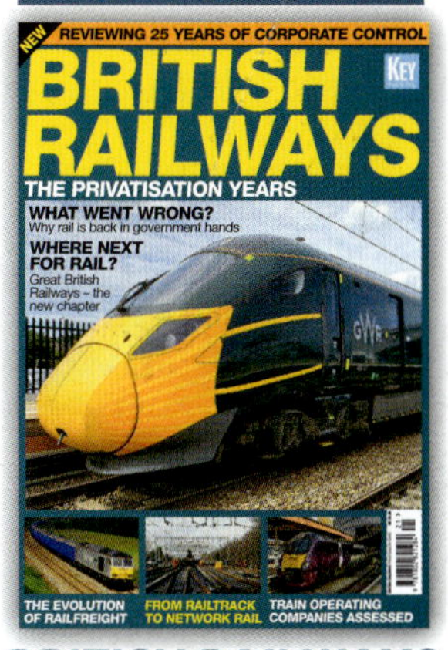

BRITISH RAILWAYS THE PRIVATISATION YEARS

£8.99 inc FREE P&P*

MODERN RAILWAYS REVIEW
The expert editorial team attempts to chart the likely way forward for the year to come.

£8.99 inc FREE P&P*

BRITAIN'S RAILWAYS IN THE 1990S
the 90's showed the greatest change in our rail system, with privatisation and booming passenger numbers.

£8.99 inc FREE P&P*

MODELLING BRITISH RAILWAYS
Locomotives of the 1990's

£8.99 inc FREE P&P*

RAIL 123
The only publication to list ALL vehicles in one easy to follow, colour coded list.

£9.99 inc FREE P&P*

MAGAZINE SPECIALS

ESSENTIAL reading from the teams behind your **FAVOURITE** magazines

HOW TO ORDER

VISIT www.keypublishing.com/shop

OR

PHONE
UK: 01780 480404
ROW: (+44)1780 480404

*Prices correct at time of going to press. Free 2nd class P&P on all UK & BFPO orders. Overseas charges apply. Postage charges vary depending on total order value.

FREE APP

Simply download to purchase digital versions of your favourite aviation specials in one handy place! Once you have the app, you will be able to download new, out of print or archive specials for less than the cover price!

IN APP ISSUES £6.99

235/23

1996

LIFE IN PRIVATE HANDS

A new business that would in due course play a major part in the rail industry was the West Coast Railway Company which was formed by the owner of the former steam shed at Carnforth. Operations initially involved spot hire of passenger rolling stock with eight coaches going on hire to South Wales and West Railways replacing those hired from Regional Railways.

The LTS franchise was due to go live in February but just before that date fraud allegations were made by London Underground concerning LTS management of joint revenue streams and the launch was put on hold. Subsequently, one of the buyout team resigned and two, still then under the control of BR, were moved to 'other duties' leading the Department for Transport to re-tender the route. It was subsequently awarded to Prism Rail, going live on May 26.

The next franchise announcement was for South Central, which was taken over by a French company with the business being renamed London & South Coast, from April 12 while National Express was to operate the very confined Gatwick Express business. The same French company Compaigne Generale des Faux, also took control of South Eastern later in the year on a 15-year term. The UK trading name was announced as Connex for both companies with a Yellow, white and blue livery that was first seen on 319021. The major commitment was to be the elimination of slam door stock by 2006. Receiving government subsidies at the outset, the award expected the balance to become payments from Connex by the end of the franchise. The East Coast Mainline set out on its tortuous life in private hands when a franchise was granted to Sea Containers Limited from April 28. The company committed to refurbishment of the high-speed train (HST) fleet, improvements via modification to the reliability of the Class 91s and the Mk 4 carriage fleet, improved on train catering and station upgrades.

M40 Trains were identified as the new owners of the Chiltern Line franchise with a plan to introduce express services from Birmingham to Marylebone and order new DMUs to operate them. Indeed, the order for new stock, the first for a DMU for 1,064 days, went to Adtranz at Derby for four Class 168s for delivery in 1998. The deal included subcontracting the maintenance of all Chiltern units to Adtranz. The next franchising announcement was for Island Lines - for services on the Isle of Wight, which passed to Stagecoach in the autumn.

Displaying the Connex livery applied to both Central and South Eastern stock from 1996, 319002 poses at Kensington Olympia in 1998. J Haydon/Colour-Rail.com

66 Britain's Railways in the 1990s

1996

Carnforth shed had long been a part of the railway scene. Following its steam era closure it became a major heritage attraction as seen here in 1975. However it gradually changed into purely an overhaul base and was closed to the public. With the formation of West Coast Railways it entered another phase of its life, once again becoming an operational part of the network. Colour-Rail.com

Privatisation continued apace with Midland Mainline going to National Express (although subject to a Monopolies and Merger Commission report), Thames Trains to a management buyout supported by Go-Ahead group and both Cardiff Railways and South Wales and West going to Prism Rail. At the outset all received government subsidies except Gatwick Express with by far the largest, at £125m being Connex South East.

A 'blame game' culture soon emerged when, for instance, a Waterloo-Weymouth electric multiple unit (EMU) was wrongly signalled at Worting Junction onto the unelectrified Salisbury route and had to wait one and a half hours to be towed back to the live rail. South West Trains blamed Railtrack for the incorrect routing and Railtrack accused the driver for not stopping when he saw the route that had been set.

Franchise requirements were complex and included the need to specify the rolling stock to be used and a plan for its replacement where deemed necessary. The 'standard' franchise period was to be seven years but in certain cases where 'new stock' proposals were made to extend that term.

Charter organisers were being frustrated by the new regime with the commercial requirements of Railtrack seeking to impose much higher charges than BR and requiring full payment up front, both increasing fares to uneconomic levels and imposing high financial risks on the organisers. The Rail Regulator had to issue a consultation paper to try and 'return commercial reality to the rail charter scene'.

Freightliner followed Res into the private sector in March. This brought into doubt the future of the terminal at Wilton on Teesside as, in order to qualify for grants, the terminal had to be located in Leeds. However, the 'big news' was that Wisconsin, the owner of Res, was also to buy Mainline, Loadhaul and Transrail, thus leaving Freightliner as the only freight competitor for the new group other than the still publicly owned Railfreight Distribution. A listing of motive power at the time of the Wisconsin takeover showed that approaching 200 locomotives dumped around the network were either withdrawn or stored, but mostly the latter comprised mainly of classes 08, 31, 33 and 47.

The all pervading 'logic' of privatisation saw the train enquiry office at Northampton start to only provide travel information about Intercity services, this despite the fact that none called at the station. The third company which had been in the initial franchise launch plan was Great Western Trains which at that time did not include most local services so effectively just all inter city services emanating from Paddington, this being another management buy-out. The franchise was granted for seven years. As well as refurbished HSTs and a commitment to maintain the sleeper services, Motorail services were promised to be re-introduced.

The Docklands Railway was the target of a large bomb that exploded on February 9 below South Quay station causing extensive damage to the railway viaduct and closing the line there for several weeks. Like BR the Government were seeking to franchise operations on the Docklands Light Railway (DLR) with a standard seven-year term and then businesses/consortia expressed an interest in operating the line.

The first sign of a change in policy for Channel Tunnel services ▶

Britain's Railways in the 1990s 67

was a statement that Nightstar services would not be introduced until 1997. No reason was stated but as no stock for these had arrived at the end of March it might have related to the time needed for training with the first set of stock not even arriving for testing until September.

London & Continental Railways won the competition to build HS1 at an estimated cost of £3bn. This company would also take over European Passenger Services Ltd.

Manchester Metrolink announced plans for the expansion of the system with a line to Eccles via Salford Quay which, subject to funding, was planned to open in 1999. The go ahead for the Croydon Tramlink was given with the awarding of the £160m contract to Tramtrack Croydon Ltd. This would include design build and operation on a 99 year lease. Unlike Manchester, the Sheffield tram system was not attracting enough passengers and making an annual loss. Under the terms of the original agreement it had to be offered for sale within two years of completion.

The Jubilee line extension from Green Park to Stratford appeared on course to open as planned in 1998 following the completion of tunnel boring.

Impersonating railway staff can end up being a serious matter. The railway 'career' of an imposter started in 1993 when he undertook two weeks of work experience at Herne Hill station, failing to return the issued uniform on completion, and indeed continuing to appear at the station. At some point he stole a drivers badge and posing as a trainee Networker driver persuaded some drivers to give him extra tuition where he

The Docklands station of South Quay was the scene of a major IRA bomb blast in 1996. It is seen here in happier times in 2005. B Perryman/Colour-Rail.com

Fresh out of the box, well almost. 08931, the first member of the class to receive English Welsh Scottish livery (EWS) is seen in Crewe Works on August 17. Just the owner's branding remains to be applied. R Hunter/Colour-Rail.com

Britain's Railways in the 1990s

1996

English Welsh Scottish proclaimed its ownership of its depots as seen here at Toton. R Hunter/Colour-Rail.com

took control of units travelling at full line speed. His false life only came to light when he reported a fire on a unit and an identity check was carried out. In court he received a two year suspended jail sentence and 100 hours community service on charges of endangering passengers and obtaining free rail travel as he also used his uniform to claim free travel to London three times per week from Margate.

The Cambrian Coast line, long being restricted to just DMU operation due to the weakness of a number of bridges seemed to have a brighter future when Railtrack announced that £1.8m would be spent on bridge repairs to allow both higher line speeds and the use of loco hauled trains.

The year ended with more franchisees announced although none took effect during the year, these being Anglia, to be run by GB Railways, West Anglia Great Northern (WAGN) by Prism Rail, Cross Country by Virgin group and Great Eastern by FirstBus. Another bus operator, MTL, gained control of the Merseyrail system.

Stock changes

The year started much as 1995 had finished with a large number of locomotive allocations being to HQ and being described as being in 'strategic reserve'.

Around this time it became increasingly difficult for the average enthusiasts to know who the owner of a locomotive was as it frequently was not the operator. For instance Freightliner sold most of its locomotive fleet to Porterbrook Leasing and then hired them back. At the same time it received locos back that had been on loan elsewhere, these remaining in Freightliner ownership.

Wisconsin announced that its trading name in the UK would be English Welsh and Scottish Railway. and displayed its new Red and Gold livery on 08921, 37051, 56089, 60017, 58033 and 73128, these having bold lettering as EW&S on the body side, its change to plain EWS in due course being the most noticeable variation in years to come. Despite the spring appearance of these locomotives the trading company did not exist until October 11. It would seem that EWS did not like names to be carried on locos in its new livery, that on 60007 having been removed. All locomotives in its fleet were having the BR double arrow removed/painted out. As well as owning locomotives, the sale to Wisconsin also included large numbers of freight vehicles. The company's announcement of a new locomotive order must have raised many eyebrows, both in respect of its size and source being for 250 American-built engines with the first due to arrive in late 1997.

EW&S set about rationalising motive power maintenance requirements by concentrating classes at one depot with Toton becoming the 'headquarters' for the loco fleet with for instance Class 60s concentrated there. Canton lost all of its Class 56s with those moving to Immingham but retained its Class 37 fleet, not that most of the allocation changes made much difference to actual loco duties.

Two Class 56s made their way to the scrap yard in the spring being 56005/26 seen at Booth Roe Metals but locomotive withdrawals were at an all-time low until near the year end when the pace quickened, at least in October, with the condemnation of eight 31s, four 33s, and 56001/9. 56024 followed in November.

English Welsh Scottish livery embarked on a programme of concentrating its motive power maintenance with each class being the primary responsibility of a single depot. Toton took on Class 60s but it was also the major overhaul centre for the whole fleet, hence the selection seen here in 1998. R Hunter/Colour-Rail.com

Coupling failures beset the Class 465s in the year with much of the fleet withdrawn pending modification leading to short formations and cancelled services. Deemed fit for traffic on June 6 was 465016 seen at Polhill. I Worland/Colour-Rail.com

A coupling failure on a Class 465/0 unit in January led to all of those plus Class 466 being grounded until safety checks had been carried which revealed that a number of units had couplers with fatigue cracks. The removal from service caused many train cancellations and reformations on the South Eastern division. Passengers were to receive compensation for the disruption caused this being paid by South Eastern who would then try to reclaim it from the lease company who in turn would be calling on ABB, as the builders, to compensate them.

London Transport received the first unit of a batch for the Jubilee line in the summer and completion of the first new set for the Northern line was due in December. Bowing out in the summer were the last '56' stock units.

Centro expressed an interest in evaluating a Parry Peoplemover on the half-mile branch between the town and Junction stations at Stourbridge.

The ranks of the Southern diesel electric multiple unit (DEMU) fleet had dwindled to just a handful. Nominally preserved however was Hastings unit 1001 also known as 201001. This was repainted in the Southern Region green used on DEMUs and EMUs and had a former 4 CEP coach put into the formation and it was then placed on hire to Hastings Diesels Ltd. Its first duty thereafter was on a railtour to Chester on August 17.

Locomotive withdrawal and ownership became ever more difficult to define as engines long since withdrawn by BR and sold 'for private use' now started to make a return visit to the network

1996

twenty years, completing nearly 70, before finally being cut up. RFS also gained a contract to supply shunting locos for use by GNER.

Services

With the concentration of the business being on establishing the new franchises it was hardly surprising that few service changes of note occurred during the year.

Ashford International station opened on January 8 although the platforms dealing with local services had already seen some passenger action. The first International service left around 07.20 in the midst of a firework display. There had been a dramatic increase in the number of services operating compared with the two and three per day seen soon after the launch but loadings appeared quite light.

Although working through the Channel Tunnel Class 92s had not been authorised to work under power on third rail lines initially. This changed in July with trial services being operated through o Willesden. The new Royal Mail depot here came into full use on September 30.

The first station opening of the year was at Yarm on February 19 and this was followed by Filton Abbey Wood on March 11. The latter was built specifically to service a large new nearby office complex to house 6000 MoD staff. The nearby station of Filton remained open but became a request stop until a proposed closure on October 1. However it was still open for two Saturday only services to call at the year end.

No doubt in preparation for franchising and to compete against the LTS route, a considerable improvement in services from Liverpool Street to Southend was being proposed for 1997 with a 30% increase in off peak trains and greatly improved travel times.

A major announcement for those living in the South East was the go ahead for a £650m Thameslink 2000 project to provide up to 24 trains per hour through the centre of London with through services from Brighton to Luton. Although dubbed '2000' it was not expected to open for six years and part of the construction would be carried out by the company building the high speed Channel Tunnel line.

Operations

Unsurprisingly the weather was cold in Scotland in December 1995 and into January 1996 with temperatures reported as falling to -20 C with some sleeper services seeing delays in excess of four hours. Passengers delayed in Glasgow were offered free tea but those at Waverley did not enjoy the luxury. The Midlands were hit on January 27/28, this snow obviously being of the 'wrong type' as it caused the failure of many Class 323s. Scotland was again hit on February 6 and 156485 on a Stranraer to Ayr working hit a 15ft snow drift in a cutting near Glen Luce in an area where there was no radio signal. A BR signalman who was travelling on the train but had one of the still rare mobile phones, then set off in a blizzard in just his 'business clothing' to climb a nearby hill to get a signal on his phone to call for help. The passengers had to be rescued by helicopter. Another snowfall, this time across East Anglia and the South East on February 19 caused more disruption, but no free tea.

The first Southern EMU, 5 WES 2402, to carry Stagecoach livery was used for a 'launch train' on February 5. 5871 worked the first service train, the start of the franchise having been brought

such as 08077 which was sold back in 1977 to Wiggins Teape and subsequently owned by RFS, but was then sent to Freightliner at Southampton, possibly on hire but more likely sold. Much confusion was caused by the TOPS system that required any loco moved via the network to be registered on the system but the true owner was not always identifiable. As it was 08077 survived almost another

A heritage unit, Class 201 1001, was restored to its original BR green livery and initially found employment on mainline charters such as its visit to Llanbradach in March 1997. N Sprinks/Colour-Rail.com

Britain's Railways in the 1990s

71

forward by the Government from the anticipated March date. Stagecoach immediately provided connecting bus services, for use only by rail passengers, from Romsey to Winchester and Bordon to Liphook. It did not take long for the other side of the equation to be seen when South West Trains announced several hundred staff redundancies.

The East Coast identity of GNER and its dark blue livery with an orange stripe was first seen on 91019 at the end of October, this being preceded on September 30 by the Great Western Trains livery launch being basically a dark green and Ivory scheme. Given the fact that power cars were frequently swapped leading to livery mismatches, along with the plans for new liveries for other franchises, this event marked the end of the whole of the HST fleet carrying a standard livery.

Bilingual station nameboards with names in Gaelic and English started to appear in parts of Scotland with the West Highland line being so adorned by July.

Another fatal accident occurred on August 8, this being at Watford when two trains worked by Class 321 units were in collision during a crossing movement with one death and 68 injured. The line was closed until 12th. There was severe damage to a number of carriages with three units involved. The subsequent shortage of stock led to one 321 being transferred in from Great Eastern duties and two Class 310 units being employed on 321 duties.

A livery that was a total departure from that seen on locomotives previously appeared on 47817, this being a white and purple scheme with 'swirls', essentially being an advert for Porterbrook, this first receiving comment in mid-May.

The first large scale Channel Tunnel emergency occurred on November 18 when a serious fire broke out on a lorry being moved through the tunnel. No one was seriously injured but there was severe damage to one of the tunnel bores and one shuttle loco, 9030, was also severely damaged. Disruption to services were expected for several weeks awaiting damage repairs.

The Class 365 units for use out of Kings Cross and on the Southern were being sent to Chart Leucon for storage while driver training was initially to be undertaken at Ramsgate along with various trials around the southern end of the East Coast route. Entry into service was reported by some as during November but others said it would not occur until January.

A shortage of EMUs saw the new Leeds and Bradford electrified service fall apart in March with a halving of services between Bradford and Skipton and the cancellation of all Leeds-Braford Foster Square trains. A full service was restored from April 29.

The follies of the reduction in the number of loco stabling places was illustrated on October 18 when the sleeper service to Inverness did not reach the Highland capital until 14.37, six hours late, having failed near Delphinine. Motherwell depot was requested to send a loco to effect the rescue but no crew was available and eventually assistance was found at Montrose. In theory no doubt Perth would have been the location of a rescue loco in the past.

The Redmire branch, which had been out of use for many months was cleared of vegetation to allow it to return to the operational railway, it being

Withdrawn by BR in the 1970s and sold for industrial use, 08077 made a mainline comeback in 1996 when it was put into service by Freightliner at Millbrook. It carries Freightliner branding on its RFS livery. Colour-Rail.com

1996

New liveries abounded in 1996. However, one that was predictable was that used by Stagecoach who used the same colours as employed on its large bus fleet, suitably adapted for application to carriages, as seen on Class 423 3411 at Reading. D Pye/Colour-Rail.com

The entry into service of the Class 365 units proved to be a long and tortured trail and in 1996 many were stored. They later went on to give good service although having a short operating life of less than twenty five years. 365535 is seen at Royston. Colour-Rail.com

used by military trains from Ludgershall to Warcop, these often conveying military vehicles.

You apparently can't please all of the people all of the time as seen when Tarmac proposed moving gravel from a pit at Levant by rail to Drayton and Porterfield which would require the relaying of the line between Levant to Fisherton Junction. The relaying of the line was opposed by cyclists because it was currently a cycle path, the council would not agree to the gravel being moved by road and an alternative proposal to dredge the gravel from the seabed was opposed by marine biologists.

Driver's lodging turns, dispensed with in the 1960s, returned for some Newcastle drivers working HST sets to Inverness.

Heritage

The Gloucestershire-Warwickshire Railway set a new target for its southwards expansion with the

Britain's Railways in the 1990s

stated aim of reaching Cheltenham Racecourse station by the year 2000.

Diesel fans were expecting great things with the return to the mainline of Deltic D9000 but its first big test run in November saw it fail at Berwick.

The Mid-Norfolk Railway made some progress towards becoming a fully functioning railway although the description of their first operations might not have inspired some to travel. Special permission was granted to run a short series of trains in December 1995 and January 1996. Because no light railway order was in place trains had to run with a BR driver on the footplate between Dereham and Yaxham. Two Class 20s 20069 and 20206, the former in undercoat, were the motive power with the train comprised of four MkII carriages in faded NSE livery. As the train heating was in operative, portable Calor gas heaters were provided on the train. None the less 600 people were carried. The BR property board agreed to sell the trackbed from Dereham to Wymondham.

The North Staffordshire Railway Co., which had been operating the line at Cheddleton morphed into the Churnet Valley Railway plc (1992), this happening in 1996 despite the company name. It was intended to buy the then disused section of the line to Oakmoor and start services over the extension before the year end.

The Great Central Railway (GCR) announced its plans to extend from Loughborough to Ruddington to join up with the existing line operated by GCR(N), 'Bridging the gap by installing bridges over the Midland mainline and a canal were seen as the major obstacle requiring funding of £3m.

The building of a train from bricks, in the form of an A4, was given the go ahead at

The North Staffordshire Railway Co Ltd changed its name to the Churnet Valley Railway in 1996. However it remained a home for North Staffordshire No. 2 as seen here in 1999.
P Chancellor/Colour-Rail.com

74

Britain's Railways in the 1990s

1996

Dark green and Ivory shades were the choice of Great Western Trains for use on all of its stock. An HST set is about to dive into Box tunnel in September 1997. R Siviter/Colour-Rail.com

Darlington with the full cost of £730,000 coming from grants.

The Sittingbourne and Kemsley Railway was able to re-open the elevated section of its line on April 21 following completion of temporary repairs.

Over the Easter period the Swanage Railway was inundated by passengers with around 8,000 carried. Such was demand that it had to close its booking office at Swanage at 13.15 on the Sunday due to overcrowding. Despite its success the line had severe financial problems. A debt of £0.5m had been 'uncovered' in 1991. Careful management had reduced the liability but it still stood at some £200,000 and a public appeal was launched to try and eliminate the debt. An army training exercise was used to prepare 400 yards of trackbed for track laying near Furzebrook.

The use of heritage lines by companies wanting to run trials and demonstrate their projects continued to grow with even BR itself having a three day total occupation of the Great Central Railway.

A start was made on recreating the Lynton & Barnstaple railway following the approval of planning permission to lay track and erect buildings at Woody Bay. It was hoped that facilities would be ready for opening in April 1997.

The Bodmin & Wenford railway expanded its sphere of operation with the opening of Boscarne station which was initially served by a DMU from Bodmin.

Plans to return services to Weardale took a step forward when Railtrack agreed to sell the 20-mile trackbed from Bishop Auckland to Eastgate for £500,000. It would be owned by a new limited company but there was no mention of where the money might be found.

Across the heritage sector, progress on some projects was rapid while others appeared to be totally dormant. This might be expected as, particularly with rolling stock and locomotives, certain projects were being undertaken by a single person or a very small group and if either funds or time ran short the schemes stalled. This could be illustrated by the ex-Barry locomotives based at the Avon Valley Railway. BR Standard tank 80104, which had made some progress, moved away to Swanage where its restoration went from slow to high speed. Conversely, 44123, 45379, 34058 and 48173 continued to languish at Bitton with apparently no progress but the application of some red oxide paint.

Plans were announced for the building of a major railway museum at Bo'ness at a cost of £7m with a lot of the funding coming from councils and Forth Valley Enterprise.

A timetabled steam hauled passenger train operated on the East Kent Railway for the first time since 1948 over the August bank holiday operated by 0-6-0T *Brookfield* on loan from Mangapps Farm.

Big plans were announced for the reconstruction of the

Some locomotive restorations moved at a fast pace, others less so. One engine in the latter category was LMS 4F 44123 which resided at the Avon Valley Railway for many years with the only apparent progress being the application of some red oxide paint. This view was taken in 2007 and it subsequently moved to new pastures but is still not in working order. P Chancellor/Colour-Rail.com

Britain's Railways in the 1990s

Almost all liveries were designed to be applied in a linear fashion. Thus the treatment applied by Porterbrook to 47817 caused a degree of controversy. It was photographed at Aller Junction heading west on September 6. R Siviter/Colour-Rail.com

The ownership of the Bure Valley Railway changed hands in 1995 and in 1996 it reported a 60% growth in passenger numbers. The terminus is seen in 2002. Colour-Rail.com

Welsh Highland Railway, where although not yet granted a Light Railway Order, some 300 tonnes of track and four locomotives were being imported from South Africa. Much of the funding for the work had come from grants including £4m from the Millenium Commission.

Intended occupants of the Brighton Works project, abandoned in 1994 made slow progress in finding new homes with 34046 *Braunton* being the last to move, going to the West Somerset Railway. That line had Minehead station flooded almost to platform level on October 28 leading to abandonment of services for the rest of the week. It was announced on December 29 that the line was to receive regular freights in 1997 conveying large rocks to bolster sea defences with those running through to Minehead.

Heritage lines, like their mainline counterparts, occasionally saw management buy outs, and this was the case at the Bure Valley Railway in 1995. The new management saw a 60% increase

4073 Caerphilly Castle was evicted from its home at the Science Museum after thirty years and was destined to go to a new museum at Swindon. However, this had not yet been built so temporary accommodation was provided by the Great Western Society at Didcot where the engine spent most of its time under cover to protect the paint work. P Chancellor/Colour-Rail.com

in passenger numbers during their first year in charge.

The Heritage site at County School attracted publicity for the wrong reasons when the local ombudsman required the lease granted by Breckland Council to be cancelled on the grounds of maladministration as the council had failed to specify any operating requirements and residents cited many instances of what they considered excessive noise and nuisance at the site.

A new home was required for 4073 *Caerphilly Castle* following a prolonged closure planned for its long-time home of the Science Museum and it moved to the Great Western Society at Didcot, possibly for up to five years.

60532 *Blue Peter* returned to the network on November 20 on test following completion of repairs following its disastrous bout of slipping at Durham the previous year.

A preservation site to fall by the wayside was that at Caerphilly with closure said to be due to continual vandalism. Much of the stock etc. was to move to the Gwili Railway. ■

Britain's Railways in the 1990s

1997

The launch of Virgin Rail saw 90002 receive what became its trade mark red. It was photographed very soon after it was applied on July 29 at Stafford. D Pye/Colour-Rail

THE TRIALS OF MULTI-OWNERSHIP

Great Western Holdings were awarded the North West Regional Franchise with a requirement to introduce 70 new diesel multiple unit (DMU) vehicles by 2,000 and provide more long distance trains with North Wales and Rochdale to London being suggested.

The Health & Safety executive indicated it expected all Mk I derived passenger stock to be removed from the network by 2007. As far as 'hauled' stock was concerned most had already been removed from stock but many were now operated on spot hire for excursions etc. but the impact would be felt most by those operating electrical multiple units (EMUs). Most of the 25Kv units were planned for renewal under franchise agreements but around 50% of all ex-Southern region EMUs would need replacement.

With a general election looming the final franchise agreements were announced over a 21-day period from February 5. The one attracting the most attention was the award of the West Coast contract to Virgin Trains and 90002, named *Mission Impossible* with a full set of stock all in the Virgin colours, as used on the Cross Country high-speed trains (XC HSTs), made an inaugural run on March 10 and the first Virgin liveried Class 47 47814 was noted at Crewe diesel depot on March 17. This deal appeared to be tied to a Railtrack commitment to spend £1.35bn on the line in upgrade work to allow a 30-minute saving between Euston and Manchester and an hour between Euston and Glasgow. However, by the year end this had already risen to £2bn. The franchise was let for 15 years and required offers to include tilting trains. It was soon announced that the latter should arrive in 2002. Virgin also advised that it intended to run through trains from both Shrewsbury and Blackpool to Euston. The size of the challenge facing Virgin was illustrated by punctuality figures on the route for London-Scotland trains with just 55.8% arriving on time in October. Regional Railways North East was vested in MTL who wished to expand Trans Pennine services but any commitment to electrification was put off. This was followed by an announcement that it intended to make 40% of the staff redundant.

National Express were awarded Central Trains and North London Railways, the former to include the Cambrian lines where no service improvements were required but likewise services could not be reduced.

Govia, the new joint venture between Go-Ahead Group and Via GTK, a French company, took the Thameslink franchise which it was noted might be renegotiated after five years if there was any disruption due to the construction of Thameslink 2000 or HS1.

National Express also gained the final franchise to be awarded, that being for Scotrail covering all services not operated by East or West coast companies and Cross Country. 38 new DMUs were

Govia was awarded the franchise to run the Thameslink service and would soon remove the livery applied to 319033 when seen at Brighton. D Pye/Colour-Rail.com

1997

pledged. Scotrail received by far the largest subsidy totalling £280m.

What were believed to be the first penalties paid for service failures under the terms of a franchise saw Stagecoach's South West Trains 'fined' £750,000 in February and £1m in March.

IRA bomb warnings, most of which turned out to be hoaxes, continued to disrupt services in the spring, particularly in the east of England.

The once very much enthusiast-orientated Steamtown centre at Carnforth closed its doors to the public to concentrate on its new role as a charter and hire company. The future of its redundant coaling tower hung in the balance.

Various criticisms of new franchise operators were made and their responses were not always seen as good public relations. Merseyrail reduced a number of peak services from six to three cars with much overcrowding being recorded. In their reply to complaints the company stated that in their view it was acceptable for 35% of passengers to have to stand for up to 15 minutes on any journey. A large number of the Class 508 units were in store being surplus to requirements.

An interesting example of privatisation at work was to be seen in Scotland where almost since the line was built from Edinburgh to Glasgow via Falkirk flooding had occurred on occasions in Winchburgh tunnel during periods of heavy rain. The BR solution to that was to divert trains via Dalmeny resulting in around a 15-minute delay. With Scotrail now proposing to double the frequency of the service and with Railtrack liable for any delay repayments, it seemed that the problem would finally be fixed at a projected cost of £700,000.

Ashchurch in Gloucestershire saw its station close in the 1960s. More than 30 years later it was provided with a new one which opened in May. Winding the clock back to 1965 D1589 can be seen working through the original one, the modern version appearing much less welcoming. Colour-Rail.com

Chiltern announced their intention to run a half hourly service from Moor Street to Marylebone and build a new station named Warwick Parkway. A new station opening took place at Ashchurch on May 30 and Rugeley Town on June 2 the latter being served by an extension of services to Hednesford.

Another illustration of the 'multi-layer' railway that had been created under privatisation was seen when a report into a freight train derailment at Bexley on February 4 was published with three companies being held responsible. The underlying cause was the poor state of the track for which Railtrack were responsible. The train was exceeding the 20 mph speed limit and was being driven by a man hired by English Welsh Scottish (EWS) from Connex who normally drove passenger trains. EWS had failed to advise him of the restricted speed applying to freight trains at the location and thirdly the train was overloaded, a fault attributed to an EWS contractor.

The first major accident involving an HST occurred at Southall on September 19, leaving seven people dead and a further 150 injured. The 10.32 Swansea-Paddington train ran into a freight train which was crossing its path on the Great Western Main Line. The HST had a faulty automatic warning system which should have been reported to Railtrack as, although such trains were at the time allowed to continue in service, there were rules that stopped the signalling of conflicting train movements in such circumstances. The driver of the HST missed two distant signals at danger as he was 'packing his bag' and only started to brake when he sighted the final signal at red resulting in a collision with the freight at 80mph. HST car 41050 was cut up on site.

The legendary fact about the Forth rail bridge was that it was a continual task to repaint it. However, an end appeared to be in sight as technology caught up with it. A repainting contract taking four years was awarded to a company that painted North Sea oil rigs and which used a system of sand blasting followed by the application of flake glass paint promising a life of 20 years.

Stock Changes

A move signalling the Europeanisation of some loco classes began when 59003, deemed surplus to Yeoman requirements in the UK due to the depressed state of the aggregates market, was loaned to Deutsche Bahn and moved to Germany.

With locomotive policy still evolving in EWS there were substantial re-allocations but no reduction in the fleet in the first two months of the year. But in March nearly all of the remaining Class 33s were withdrawn with 17 condemned. The Waterman Railways fleet of Class 47s were sold to a new operating company, Fragonset Railways with 47703 being the first to appear carrying their name. Just two Class 141 DMUs remained in service in April with storage of the class split between Heaton and Doncaster.

Great North Eastern Railways (GNER) asked for quotations for the supply of two 140 kph tilting trains for delivery in 1999 with an option for up to 45 extra units.

The start of services using Class 365 units allowed the transfer of the first Class 317 units to the LTS route.

Deemed surplus to requirements 59003 was destined to leave the country for more than 20 years. Here it heads an aggregates train at Botley in 1994. Colour-Rail.com

Britain's Railways in the 1990s

79

When Prism rail took over the London Tilbury and Southend (LT&S) line to Southend it was worked by an aging fleet of Class 302 EMUs. As a stop gap measure before the arrival of new stock a number of surplus Class 317 units were drafted in. Carrying no branding and a livery akin to some former Regional Railways stock 317302 stands at Barking. I Thomas/Colour-Rail.com

New EMUs for the LTS line were ordered from Adtranz which along with a maintenance contract the projected cost was to be £200m. There were to be 44 sets.

Prototype electric 89001 was readied for a return to front line duties at Brush Loughborough and departed in GNER livery on March 3 and worked its first revenue earning duty on the 27th with a Kings Cross-Bradford train. The company were very quick to 'relivery' its motive power with all Class 91s and their HST power cars completed by August.

The importance of Brush as a loco repair and refurbishment facility continued to grow with for instance six EWS Class 56s on site in December.

For many months GNER had hired in locomotives to boost its loco fleet to cover for unavailable Class 91s and this practice started spreading with Anglia needing to supplement its Class 86 fleet. The problem was they needed push-pull fitted engines but most replacements – being Class 86/4 rather than 86/2 – were not fitted. It sometimes meant that two locos were needed to carry out the work done by one 86/2 as run round facilities and schedules did not allow the incoming loco to take the booked return train.

Plans for new stock for the Gatwick Express franchise were announced being for eight EMUs with eight cars built at Alstholm's Metro Cammell plant with delivery due in May 1999. Other rolling stock orders began to emerge with Class 357 EMUs for the LTS line, stock for Waterloo-Reading services, which came out as Class 458 and Turbostar DMUs for Midland Mainline.

The first non-UK built units of any type other than the Channel Tunnel stock arrived from Spain in the spring for the Heathrow Express service. The EMUs were designated as Class 332.

With many withdrawn locomotives having been in store for months and even years some had deteriorated to the stage where they could not be moved easily. There was also a requirement that anything that moved on Railtrack lines had to be registered on the Total Operating Process System (TOPS) as fit to move. This led to a number of locomotives being cut up where they stood with a new contractor M R J Phillips doing most of the work. This included the demise of 56001 at Cardiff Canton. Old Oak Common saw frequent activity with the demise of eight Class 47s.

EWS strengthened its grip on the UK freight market by the acquisition of Railfreight Distribution, leaving just Freightliner and a very small DRS as its only potential competitors. The latter started the expansion of its locomotive fleet with the purchase of a further 12 Class 20s previously owned by BRT Racal and 37607-12 from Eurostar, four of which promptly went on hire to Freightliner. EWS continued with its maintenance rationalisation programme by transferring all of its remaining Class 31s to Bescot and sold some Class 47s to Freightliner. The latter seemingly went against increased volumes of freight moved by EWS which was re-instating engines from store to cope. Bolstering the EWS fleet were the National Power 59s 59201-6 which transferred across in September.

The long drawn out saga of Class 365s entry into service saw the final unit 365541 delivered on September 5 but many of the class were still not in use by the year end.

The disposal and ownership of redundant motive power became yet more complex when the second-hand market was entered by Harry Needle who in the coming years purchased many locomotives. The challenge came where his stock was stored at various heritage lines leading magazines to report an engine sold for preservation when in fact it was simply stored on behalf of Harry Needle and even in some cases loaned to the lines for operational use. Similarly reports of locos sold to network operators from his stock in fact later turned out to be hire agreements.

One of the more forgotten elements of railway management was the provision of snow ploughs, this on the 'new' railway being under the care of Railtrack. Long gone were the days when almost every engine shed had a snow plough that it could attach to the front of a steam engine and the inherited stock of ploughs comprised of two snow blowers, ten modern Beilhack patrol ploughs and 42 more ancient machines from which Railtrack selected 22 for upgrading giving a contract for the work to RFS at Doncaster for completion during 1998. The snow blowers were to be found at Inverness and Stewarts Lane with nearly all the other ploughs spread across the network from the south of Scotland down the east side of the country with the furthest south at Stewarts Lane. Only Wigan and Cardiff were used on the west side.

To help overcome the perennial shortage of Class 91s on East Coast services, experimental electric 89001 was hired and received GNER livery. It looks ready to depart at Kings Cross on July 29. Colour-Rail.com

80

Britain's Railways in the 1990s

1997

GNER acquired a number of MKIII carriages that had been built as sleepers and these were to be re-engineered at Rosyth Dockyard to HST specification cars to augment existing sets.

Services

This turned out to be another year where service changes were minimal.

The first retrenchment of the Channel Tunnel offering was seen with the withdrawal of the Edinburgh-Waterloo HST service due to Eurostar not renewing the contract. The service from Cardiff had ceased in 1996, thus now making Waterloo an HST free zone again. The London terminus was however served again but most unexpectedly via a Class 158 from Manchester that ran via Hereford and the Severn Tunnel on its way to the capital. The stock was provided by Wales & West passenger services under their new Alpha Line brand name.

Eurostar introduced a trial service running on Saturdays only to Bourg St. Maurice for those wishing to visit the French Alps. An accountant's report suggested that Sleeper services from Edinburgh through the tunnel would never be financially viable.

The provision of Summer Sunday trains from Exeter to Okehampton was repeated for a third year with passenger numbers consistently rising to the extent that there was a suggestion that a Saturday service should also be provided.

Very mixed messages on fares were being advertised with, for instance, South West Trains and Central advertising price reductions while Virgin was raising Anglo Scottish Super Saver fares by 15%. Then there were the first signs of fragmentation of universal tickets with West Anglia Great Northern (WAGN) trying to tempt customers away from GNER services on the Peterborough to London line by offering annual season tickets for use on WAGN only at a price 25% lower than an 'any operator' one.

Some lateral thinking by Great Western Trains saw a two for one offer provided as long as the claimant had three 'mast heads' from the Daily Telegraph newspaper.

The summer timetable saw the start of the promised Connex run service from Gatwick to Rugby taking Class 319 units into the heart of West Midlands territory. Other proposals in the area came from Central Trains to provide through services from Birmingham to Stanstead and Norwich and indeed one through train per day to the latter did start with the summer timetable.

Many areas had seen a boost in freight traffic although it was unclear if that was due to mainly to

The first EMUs built on the continent for use on the national network were the Class 332s built specifically for Heathrow Express duties. 332010 stands at Paddington. Most members of the class have already been consigned to the scrap heap. D Pye/Colour-Rail.com

The year saw eight Class 47s cut up at Old Oak Common shed. Dumped there since 1991, 47465 was consigned to history in April of 1997. This shot was taken two years earlier. Colour-Rail.com

National Power was a short lived owner of Class 59s transferring their fleet to EWS in 1997. The latter lost little time in making their ownership clear by applying their livery as seen on 59205. Colour-Rail.com

Britain's Railways in the 1990s

Railtrack initiated a review of the snow plough fleet, removing some from stock while overhauling and re-allocating others. One machine definitely not going for scrap was rotary plough ADB968501 seen when apparently new, at Eastleigh in 1992. R Hunter/Colour-Rail

Until very recently services from Exeter to Okehampton were run only in the summer and then not every year, but they ran in 1997 and again the following year which is when 150241 was photographed at Okehampton. I Thomas/Colour-Rail.com

the activities of a privatised system or an upturn in the economy. Coal traffic was down overall with an almost complete move from UK-mined traffic to imported. Steel services were definitely on the up both for import and export with new facilities constructed at Hull and Boston. On a much smaller scale, timber movements had returned and aggregates were recovering. However, it was the intermodal sector that saw a major growth in traffic with Felixstowe shipping up to 900 containers per day by rail.

Operations

As noted previously, Richard Branson entered the railway arena with his franchise to operate Cross Country trains and an HST set was 'reliveried' for the launch in January. The initial repaint included XC branding alongside the Virgin name with HST cabs carrying yellow roofs back to a line with the cab door, Power cars started to receive 'appropriate' names such as 43098 which became *Lady in Red*.

Another new livery was that applied to Strathclyde sponsored stock this being described as Carmine and Cream although the red shade was darker than that previously used by BR. It was first recorded on 314215 in September. Some class 319 units working for Connex were refurbished to include First Class accommodating and redesignated as 319/2.

A small number of aging Class 121 bubble cars wandered far from their original Western Region territory to take up duties on the Sudbury branch in Suffolk although poor reliability led to bus substitutions on a number of occasions.

Deltic D9000 heralded a return to service with a railtour starting at Kings Cross on January 2, going through to Hull. On July 23 it worked its first scheduled passenger service when it was hired by Virgin to work 09.05 Paddington Manchester as far as New Street and a return working as far as Reading due to a shortage of Class 47s and it was used on similar duties in August. It continued to see occasional use by Virgin but by the autumn it was common practice for them to have at least one Fragonset loco covering their duties.

The fortunes of the Settle and Carlisle line seemed on the up with much increased volumes of freight and the need to remain open on at least three nights per week.

A very unusual working took place on July 16 when a two coach HST set plus two power cars replaced a Class 158 unit between Glasgow and Carstairs, the HST being formed of GNER liveried

1997

EMUs working in the Strathclyde area received a new livery which harked back to the 1950s with a near match for Carmine and Cream. 314208 shows off the scheme at Glasgow Central. K Fairey/Colour-Rail.com

43106 two Mk III carriages one in InterCity livery, the other Virgin and Intercity liveried 43065.

Something that would have been unthinkable ten years earlier was the collection of liveries on display at Millerhill on January 9 being EWS red, Transrail grey, Loadhaul orange, 56104 in coal sector livery, 60095 in two tone grey, 37351 in Engineers livery, two 08 shunters in blue and grey liveried 09205.

Travels through Kent in recent years had not been noted for the number of locomotives that could be noted. Nonetheless, on October 18 a journey from Charing Cross to Folkestone allowed the traveller to see 53 of 12 classes in ten liveries although the 18 Class 92s parked up at Dollands Moor boosted the total considerably.

It appeared that there was very little that was new on our railways with frequent train cancellations both in the former Southern area around London and in the northwest due to a shortage of drivers.

The importance of certain industrial customers was highlighted by the painting of two Class 60s 60006/33 in a unique light blue livery for British Steel, the two being 'launched at a special ceremony at the Appleby Frodingham steel works on July 17. The names *Scunthorpe Ironmaster* and *Tees Steel Express* were carried. Milk trains briefly returned to the network, these running from Penrith to Cricklewood with traction provided by DRS Class 20s but they only loaded to piggy back road four tanks daily.

A West Coast set of rolling stock complete with DVT 82113 worked right through to Penzance on July 1 when they were used instead of an HST to form the 09.10 Edinburgh Penzance hauled by 47822.

The joys of attending the Glastonbury pop festival were noted at both Bristol and Westbury where clean-up operations had to be launched to remove large quantities of mud left by returning travellers from the event.

Privatisation appeared to do little for service reliability at the time with the East Coast mainline reported as having major disruption on seven days between January 13 and 25. Complaints where parallels can be seen today saw Southwest Trains criticised for service cancellations due to driver shortages and South Eastern for overcrowding following a reduction in train lengths to avoid continued hiring of some 4 CEPs.

Some problems took a long time to resolve and in particular the cabling fault reported at Edinburgh Waverley in 1994, the full range of routing options only being restored in February.

After many years with just a minimal passenger service the Central Wales line was intensively used for four days between March 28 and 31 as a diversionary route for freight from South Wales due to a bridge being renewed at Bridgend with some freights even being worked by pairs of Class 56s.

With 59003 declared surplus for aggregate workings attention turned to finding additional duties for the other Class 59s and the type was put to work on iron ore trains between Port Talbot and Llanwern.

The preserved Hastings diesel electric multiple unit (DEMU) set 1001 made what would in due

A new livery was unveiled for 60006/33 to mark their employment on duties for British Steel. 60033 looks like it has just received the fresh coat of paint at Hither Green on October 4. Colour-Rail.com

Britain's Railways in the 1990s

Some of the few Summer Saturday extras that remained in the timetable used West Coast mainline coaching stock. It used to travel to the West Country complete with its driving van trailer (DVT). 47651 heads one such set at Cockwood. R Siviter/Colour-Rail.com

course turn out to be a regular occurrence when it was hired to work a timetabled train , that being the 08.24 Portsmouth Harbour-Cardiff and return on March 15.

A large new freight site near Daventry, forever known as DIRFT - Daventry International Rail Freight Terminal, officially became part of the network on 20 April. 08951 was the first shunter to work there and 47525 worked the first arrival, that being from Milan.

EWS opened a new loco fuelling and stabling point at Warrington Arpley and closed similar facilities at Wigan Springs Branch.

From April 1 West Coast Railways supplied the coaching stock used for some Cardiff Valleys services while in North Wales, hired carriages in chocolate and cream appeared in mixed formations with existing Regional Railways liveried carriages.

A new livery to emerge was Silverlink, the new name for North London Railways, this being applied to Classes 313 and 321 working north London on the West Coast route with 313134 and 321429 being the first recorded on July 18.

Showing that the boom in passenger numbers was not confined to the south of the country, Railtrack announced plans to increase capacity at Leeds by adding four new platforms and a new entrance. The company had announced that the present station was working to capacity.

Heritage

The A1 Steam Locomotive Trust continued to receive grants towards the building of 60163 and hoped to move into its shed at Hopetown Works, Darlington in May and would then transfer the already constructed loco frame from Tyseley via a display at the National Railway Museum in April.

The future of Barrow Hill shed seemed assured after it was purchased by Chesterfield Borough Council in January but the Museum of Army Transport at Beverley closed due to lack of funds.

B1 61264 returned to steam at the Great Central Railway in April although in non authentic Apple Green livery.

Plans for the closure of the GWR Museum in Swindon were announced with a replacement being planned using a nearly £8m lottery fund grant, this to be situated in the old R shop on part of the works land with an opening planned for 1999.

At Peak Rail it was announced that an agreement had been reached with Dr Tony Marchington, owner of *Flying Scotsman* to develop a comprehensive maintenance facility for his stock at Rowsley, this being linked to network access via the extension of Peak Rail lines to Buxton. The extension from Darley Dale to Rowsley opened in April.

Two train running was to be introduced at the Swanage Railway from July with the opening of a new signal box at Harman's Cross. Passenger numbers using the Norden Park & Ride site were such that the council started work on extension to the car park to double its capacity.

Some North Wales coast services were regularly comprised of hired in locomotives and coaching stock and the latter included some in chocolate and cream livery. One such vehicle is coupled next to 37414 at Bangor. R Siviter/Colour-Rail.com

84   *Britain's Railways in the 1990s*

1997

The North Norfolk Railway held a diesel gala which employed not just mainline types but also diesel shunters including 12131 shown here. P Chancellor/Colour-Rail.com

The West Somerset Railway played host to Yeoman's 59004 in February to allow German driver training to take place prior to the move of 59003 to that country. The trains running from Merehead bringing rocks for bolstering the sea defences started in January. It was originally intended to run one per day but it has since proved possible for two to be provided. Motive power used to date had always been a Class 37. It was anticipated the work might last for up to five years.

A sign of how quickly time seems to pass was the Maybach Returns gala on May 18, marking 20 years since the final diesel hydraulics were withdrawn. Motive power included D821/32, D1041, D7017/75 D9551 and interloper D7523.

Another line with an impressive diesel line up was the North Norfolk Railway which for a gala on June 14/15 turned out D3935, 12131, D8001 20048, D5207,

The Mid-Hants railway sought to recreate activities on the line from the last months of steam traction and renumbered some of its locos to add to the authenticity. One to be so treated was S15 30506 which appeared as classmate 30512 and is seen arriving at Medstead & Four Marks. P Chancellor/Colour-Rail.com

The Mid-Norfolk Railway was in the process of restoring its long line and re-opened Dereham station in 1997. However it would struggle to ever recreate this scene as the MCW design of DMU has long been extinct but the Derby one does have representatives at the Midland Railway Centre. This view dates from 1968. Colour-Rail.com

D5386 and D6732, the latter being the only operational Class 37 in preservation at the time.

The Welshpool and Llanfair Railway received perhaps the largest grant so far to an operational line from the Heritage Lottery Fund totalling £495,000 to restore the line to its original state when opened in 1902. It was planned to coincide with its centenary.

Work was under way relaying the Welsh Highland Railway assisted by the arrival of a track laying machine that would allow up to 200' of track to be laid daily with the working party being based at Dinas. A planning application had been made for the extension to reach the Ffestiniog station at Porthmadoc and three hundred objections had been lodged.

A recent feature of some railway special events was the recreation of specific happenings and in early July the Mid-Hants Railway put on a 30th anniversary of closing gala which involved the renumbering of its locos to those that appeared on the final few days of the line's BR life so long lost 30512, 31875, 34102 and 73092 all appeared and a further recreation was that of a scrap train saw D6593 hauling 76017 minus connecting rods on its 'final journey'.

Dereham station on the Mid Norfolk Railway re-opened on July 26.

The Bluebell Railway purchased the trackbed of the line from Horsted Keynes to Ardingly as a long term safeguard although all efforts remained focused on reaching East Grinstead.

The end of heritage operations by the Great Western Trust appeared to be in sight when Railtrack refused to renew the lease that the group had to occupy and operate from Southall shed.

A long term plan to link the Mid and North Norfolk Railways was proposed. ■

Britain's Railways in the 1990s

The derelict locomotive maintenance shed at Carlisle was acquired by DRS to accommodate its growing locomotive fleet. Today it is perhaps more busy than ever and in July 2019, 66426 was on the jacks inside the main shed. P Chancellor/Colour-Rail.com

1998

CLASS 66 BOOST FOR FREIGHT

A £2m scheme to make Birmingham New Street a more pleasant station was launched, this mainly being for cosmetic improvements at platform level. It had a minimal effect on the infamous black hole.

A start was made on the rejuvenation of the Chiltern route with a new station at Haddenham & Thame being built that could accommodate the redoubling of the track on the section through to Princes Risborough. As part of this project and with the line closed Chiltern trains from Banbury ran into Paddington for one week in January.

Following on from substantial fines imposed on Stagecoach for poor service, Connex South Eastern was fined £0.5m for service failings in late 1997. However, in a statement the latter advised that as most of the delays were due to track faults and leaves on the line it would be claiming a large proportion of it back from Railtrack. In the autumn Connex announced that the management and administration of South East and Central franchises would be merged.

The HS1 line proposal looked like running into problems when the winning bidder London & Continental Railways advised that it was having problems raising the required investment capital.

Official bodies took a long time to come to conclusions but, nearly 12 months after being awarded the Scotrail franchise, National Express was told it would need to sell its competing coaching business Scottish CityLink.

Re-instatement of an East West rail link had featured on a number of occasions and with support from Railtrack, plus all the councils along the way, the government wanted to see a detailed business plan. The proposed route was from Felixstowe to Cambridge thence Hitchin, Sandy, Bletchley and Oxford to Swindon. Backers claimed that just ten miles of track needed to be put in place.

After a long time in an 'almost finished' state the new Royal Mail depot at Shieldmuir opened for rail business in January.

Due to growth in business Freightliner opened a new facility at Wentloog replacing its Pengam site in Cardiff where there was no room for expansion. EWS signed a contract to provide all of the motive power for engineering trains. What was to become an ongoing challenge was the size of shipping containers with that industry increasing the size with a new standard of 9ft 6ins replacing 8ft 6ins. The UK loading gauge was such that very few lines could accommodate the larger size and both wagon design and gauge enhancements would be needed to allow the carrying of these in the coming years. Freightliner continued to expand its facilities opening a servicing point in Crewe Basford Hall yard and taking over the facilities at Ipswich. Another fuelling point was planned for the Southampton Maritime yard.

A new station at Luton Airport had been under construction for some time but work came to a halt when it was discovered

Some Class 508 units started life on the Southern region before being transferred to Merseyside. Service revisions rendered a number of them redundant in the North West and they returned whence they came and into the Connex fleet. 508202 was seen at Maidstone West in February 1999. D Ovenden/Colour-Rail.com

86 Britain's Railways in the 1990s

1998

that Railtrack had failed to negotiate an access agreement with local landowners.

DRS opened its flagship depot at Carlisle by taking over the former diesel depot at Kingmoor which had long been closed and overrun with vegetation.

The first major takeover of a franchisee took place when Great Western Trains Holdings was acquired by First Group as Firstbus had now become, this including the Northwest trains franchise whilst Go-Ahead bought out the 34.8% of Victory Railway Holdings, owner of Thames Trains, that it did not already own to gain complete control of the company while Alstholm gained ownership of Eastleigh works via the purchase of Wessex Traincare.

Work was noted under way in April on the Croydon Tramlink project with construction of the Therapia Way depot and flyovers at Wandle Park and Mitcham Junction progressing well. The first trams arrived on September 14 and limited test runs started in October. However, at London Transport the proposed opening of the Jubilee line extension had been put back by one year due to problems with the Westinghouse signalling system. Subsequently, the project director resigned and an American firm, Betchel, were hired to complete the project. Meanwhile, in the Midlands the first tram car was received from Italy via Immingham docks in February. It took until September for units to venture out onto the system and permission to start driver training came on October 15, meaning that the planned start of services in that month would not be achieved. A new date in January was proposed.

The Docklands Light Railway (DLR) was owned by the London Docklands Development Corporation, but this organisation ceased to exist from April 1 with ownership of DLR passing to the state. Plans were approved for an extension to London City Airport. Railtrack was on occasions criticised over running projects but LT may have created a record when it completed work at Mornington Crescent station which reopened after five-and-a-half years of rebuilding, the original target had been 15 months.

Stagecoach took over operation of Sheffield Supertram in May. Nottingham became the latest city to propose returning trams to its streets. However, a dark cloud was cast over the future of light rail schemes following a statement by Deputy Prime Minister John Prescott, as a new White Paper concluded that bus priority schemes represented much better value than light rail. At the time schemes had been proposed for Leeds, south Hampshire, Bristol, Edinburgh as well as Nottingham and extensions to the Tyne Wear and Manchester systems. That said, planning approval was granted for an extension of the Manchester system to Ashton under Lyne. Not to be deterred The New Edinburgh Tramway Co was launched on September 22 with the intention of returning trams to that city by 2001. The extension of the Tyne Wear Metro to Sunderland was authorised at the year end.

Another announcement from 'two Jags' Prescott established the Strategic Rail Authority citing that the current organisation was failing to put the passenger first. New people would be appointed to all the key positions including those of Franchise Director, BR Board chairman and the Rail Regulator. It was expected that it would be early 2000 before the new system would be in place which in due course would pave the way for the micromanagement of the industry by the Government via much more stringent franchise conditions. On October 5 contracts were let for the construction of HS1.

Another franchise restructure concerned Virgin Trains, which when formed held only a 49% share with various venture capitalists having the rest. Under

The first recorded public use of a Parry People Mover was at Bristol in May 1998. There was no identity for the machine recorded in the railway press. Another unidentified example was found at the Severn Valley Railway at Highley in 2021.
P Chancellor/Colour-Rail.com

Britain's Railways in the 1990s

87

A new Freightliner livery was seen for the first time when 47356 emerged in rebuilt form as 57001, although there was little evidence of the changes made to the casual observer. It was to be found at Toton shed in August 1998 during an open weekend. A Woolford/Colour-Rail.com

the fresh deal Virgin increased its share to 51% with Stagecoach acquiring the other 49%. The Government approved the change subject to a number of stringent requirements being added to the franchise agreement.

The former carriage works at York was taken over by Thrall-Europa for wagon building and maintenance and their first wagon, a 100 tonne steel coil carrier was outshopped on July 28. The wagon moved to Thornaby where it was stripped down again for training purposes.

West Coast Railway company, that had been operating the Jacobite since 1995 on a hire agreement obtained their own train operator's licence late in the year which would allow direct negotiations with Railtrack to operate the service in future years. Unusually, the operation ran into trouble in September when both of the allocated engines, 48151 and 75014, failed and even a diesel

The arrival of 168001 for Chiltern Trains marked the end of a long period when no DMUs were newly produced. It was out on test at Rotherby on April 28. Edward Ward/Colour-Rail.com

1998

could not be substituted on some days due to the lack of a driver.

Concerns about traffic density were expressed concerning the Castlefield Junction-Manchester Piccadilly section where trains accessing the Trafford Park freightliner terminal had to mingle with a passenger services, a state of affairs still not resolved today.

Operations

The year opened with multiple working equipment being fitted to 60005/10.

London Transport began using its new 1996 stock on public services from January 6.

The claimed first public use of a Parry People Mover began on May 21 in Bristol to run from Prince Street bridge to the dock containing the SS *Great Britain*.

The railway press at the time carried much news about the orders for new rolling stock which later failed to materialise. One such was an order from Virgin valued at £335m being for 43 tilting diesel electric multiple units (DEMUs) plus 34 push-pull locomotive and coach formations. The first manifested itself as Class 220 although the push-pull locos and stock never materialised. An order for 55 Virgin West Coast tilting trains was valued at £1bn.

A number of Class 508 electric multiple units (EMUs) that were redundant from Merseyside duties were refurbished and renumbered for use by Connex South East with the first entering traffic on the Sheerness branch on August 3. Units were renumbered in the 508/2 series in numerical order thus making it difficult to establish their former identities.

Forty-seven Class 170 DMUs to be built by Adtranz at Derby were said to be on order for customers Midland Main Line, Central Trains, ScotRail and Anglia. Yet another order was for Class 333 EMUs, to replace the existing stock on the Leeds & Bradford to Skipton line, the order being placed with Seimens. Yet more orders were confirmed with 40 Class 334 EMUs for Scotrail by Alstholm and 44 Class 357s for LTS Rail by Adtranz. Adtranz received an additional order for 30 Class 375s for Connex South Eastern, this sudden abundance of orders giving the train building industry a major challenge after several years with very little to do. Projected delivery dates ranged from October 1998 into the next century.

A re-engineering of some Class 47 locos got under way for Freightliner to produce what became Class 57 with 47356 being the first conversion, the loco having been in store for some two years. Re-entry to traffic came in July with a further five conversions authorised. The rebuild saw the fitting of a GM 2500hp engine along with many other modifications. The quite dull original Freightliner livery was replaced by a dark green and yellow scheme.

Perhaps the most significant event of the year in the freight industry was the arrival in April of 66001 which was shipped to Immingham. It quickly moved to Toton, then to Chester, back to Toton and finally to Derby Technical Centre all before the end of the month. It was noted on

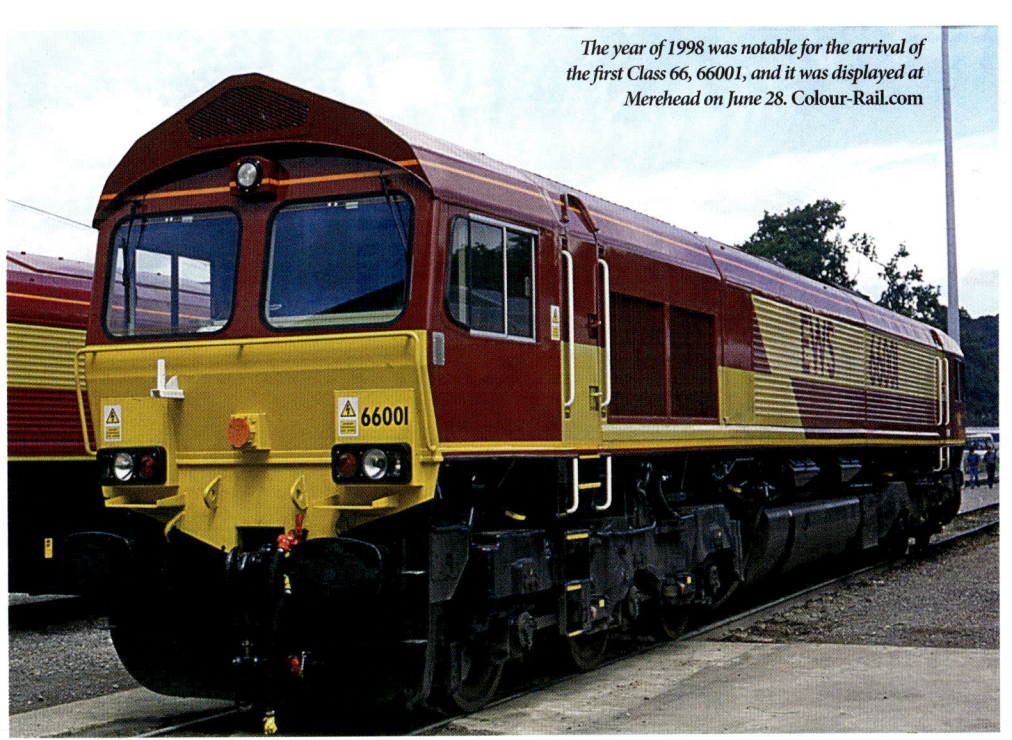

Class 03 hung to life on a thread with 03179 surviving its class mates by a number of years thanks to use on departmental duties on the Isle of Wight. Finally declared surplus there it found a new home as a depot shunter at Hornsey. In its final full year on the island it was photographed at Ryde on April 18 1998. Colour-Rail.com

The year of 1998 was notable for the arrival of the first Class 66, 66001, and it was displayed at Merehead on June 28. Colour-Rail.com

89

The Class 37/9s, as test bed engines, were always likely to be susceptible to early withdrawal and the end came for the subclass in 1998. They had seen regular use in South Wales and 37901 displayed its Transrail livery in the sun at Newport in 1996. D Pye/Colour-Rail.com

trials around Buxton at the end of May. Almost coinciding with the arrival of the 66 was the first Class 168 DMU for Chiltern to break the drought of deliveries for both locos and DMUs. The pace of disposal of redundant locomotives for cutting up appeared to be quickening with 13 – all Class 47s – cleared out from Tinsley in January and February. Fragonset and Harry Needle between them purchased ten Class 31s followed by five Class 33s. Fragonset initially operated primarily from the Tyseley premises of the former steam shed and shared with the Birmingham Railway Museum where some of their Class 31s were noted on September 11 with 31452 being in Fragonset livery.

An interesting reallocation of a locomotive concerned Class 03, for long extinct on the mainland but two examples were still nominally in stock on the Isle of Wight being 03079 and 03179 although both in store. 03079 was sold for preservation but 03179 was purchased by West Anglia Great Northern (WAGN) for use as a depot shunter at Hornsey.

The final use of Class 302 units appeared to be in July, these having given sterling service on the London Tilbury and Southend (LTS) route for many years.

The Southall accident of 1997 had seen high-speed train (HST) car 41050 cut up and subsequently 41049 was condemned. To replace these two vehicles sleeper coaches stored cars 40505/11 were sent to Adtranz for conversion to First Open layout.

Two new classes broke cover within a few days of each other, first to appear on October 31 being Class 458 EMU 8001 known as Juniper sets, these for Waterloo-Reading duties. November 4 saw a press launch of a carriage from 170102 at Derby. The 458s were to encounter a number of problems, starting with the fact that there were no seats fitted as the supplier had gone out of business.

Class 66 arrivals reached 66048 by the year end and it was noted they were being put into service almost immediately after arrival on the dockside rather than the horrendously drawn out testing and checking procedures seen with British built locos.

Concealed from those observing trains were the frequent changes in pool codes at this time, this in most cases being purely an administrative item but leading to large reallocation lists in the magazines each month.

The Class 321 unit involved in the Watford accident two years previously returned to the network at the year end, However very little of the original unit remained in as much as one car had received a ready built spare body but the other three cars were almost built from scratch at Crewe with just some components and items like seats re fitted from the original unit, the unit being 321420.

It appeared that Freightliner were happy with their 'new' Class 57s as an order was placed for a further twelve conversions.

Classes 33 and 37/9 nominally became extinct at the year-end but with the motive power pool in a state of flux no one would be surprised if they resurfaced in the coming months.

Services

The trend towards the elimination of buffet facilities on former Southern electric lines was accelerated by the withdrawal of these on the Brighton line. Of ten trains noted on the final day of operation just two had the buffet open.

Franchisees began to increase services in line with their charter

Services to London from the northwest were briefly operated by Northernwestern using both Class 158s and 322s. 322484 is seen passing Stafford on one such duty on August 14. Colour-Rail.com

1998

Poor passenger numbers on a Summer Saturdays only train from Hastings as far as Birmingham were transformed when Virgin hired in D9000 to work the duty in both 1998 and 1999. It was caught on film at Kings Sutton on August 21 1999.
R Siviter/Colour-Rail.com

37701 was busy rescuing high-speed trains on June 7 and at least one photographer caught up with it at Plymouth. Given that it was summer, he must have been on the 'late shift' to capture it after dark.
Colour-Rail.com

commitments, an example being the Liverpool Street to Shenfield service running every ten minutes and on the Great North Eastern Railway (GNER) a number of additional trains operated to Leeds and Newcastle. Regular services from Birmingham to Stanstead Airport, run by Central Trains, also started and Cross Country now provided an hourly service from Newcastle to Birmingham. New services run by North Western trains from Rochdale with a Class 158 and Manchester with Class 322s went through to Euston, these transferred from Stanstead Express duties.

Class 158 units were also used by Cross Country to provide services from Blackpool to Portsmouth. Due to a shortage of Class 322s, 309627 was used on a service to London on August 31.

The marketing name Northern Spirit was adopted and applied to units working for ▶

Britain's Railways in the 1990s 91

To cover a shortage of DMUs both Class 37/4s and 50031 plus stock were hired in to work Rhymney-Cardiff services in both 1998 and 1999. 50031 is seen near Bargoed on August 28 1999. C Wilkinson/Colour-Rail.com

the former Regional Railways North East in the spring.

Although 168001-5 were scheduled to enter service as three-car sets on May 26 only 168001 made that date. Following the arrival of the final unit, five additional centre coaches were supplied to make them all up to four-car formations. However this was immaterial as Railtrack failed to complete the track work and signalling between Princes Risborough and Bicester and so the new service for which the 168s were required was postponed for six weeks.

The first station opening of the year was Brunswick between Liverpool Central and St Michaels on March 16. It being near the site of the engine shed that closed in the 1960s. It was followed by Dalgetty Bay on March 28. The third and final stage of the Robin Hood line opened on May 11.

Cross Country provided a summer Saturdays only service from Birmingham to Ramsgate which ran through to Edinburgh on its return, this usually being lightly loaded south of Birmingham. In an inspired item of promotion Virgin hired D9000 to work these services south of Birmingham. Naturally passenger numbers increased dramatically.

A public notice transferred the ownership of the line from East Leake to Loughborough from Railtrack to the GCR(N) heritage line. The line saw use for the first time in over ten years when a delivery of sulphurised gypsum was made near Rushcliffe Halt with 60074 in charge.

Although DRS had been operating for many months the movement of nuclear waste continued to be handled by EWS. It was announced in August that there would be a gradual transfer of the work to DRS for completion by March 1999.

Operations

Overhead electrification came to Paddington on January 19 with the launch of the Heathrow Express service although initially it only ran to Heathrow Junction where a temporary terminus had been constructed with passengers conveyed to the airport in dedicated buses.

The success of Felixstowe as a container port continued with a planned move of Maersk Line business from Southampton, possibly requiring an additional

92

1998

A depot was dying and with just a month left until closure 47229 stood outside Tinsley shed on March 4. The loco was transferred to Bescot in the same month but was put to store in the autumn. Believed not to have worked again it was bought by Fragonset but it would be another nine years before it was cut up. R Hunter/Colour-Rail.com

five trains per day. It did not give an overall increase in the number of containers moved by rail but put more strain on the already single track branch line from Ipswich. Railtrack announced an £8m scheme to enhance signalling and the track layout on the branch. Despite being Freightliner services a number of duties from the port had been worked by EWS Class 56s but these stopped on May 23 with Freightliner supplying Class 47s for these turns.

All of the revisions of locomotive pools by EWS seen in 1997 resulted in sightings of formerly 'rare' engines across the UK. When allocated to the three original companies engines only occasionally strayed from their regular duties but for instance with EWS putting all of its Class 60s in one pool 96 of the one hundred class members were recorded at Thornaby in 1997. However this did not account for the arrival of 90017 at the shed on January 4, this loco having been removed from a mail train at Darlington and then towed to Thornaby for repair.

Locomotive hauled duties on the Rhymney to Cardiff route were increased from January using a hired 37/4 and ex Waterman Railways carriages. Travel by enthusiasts on some of these services became even more desirable when Class 50 50031 was drafted in to help for a nominal eight weeks.

Almost since new HST sets with only one working power car were not allowed over the South Devon banks without an assisting locomotive and this requirement persisted usually being covered with a Class 47 but ➤

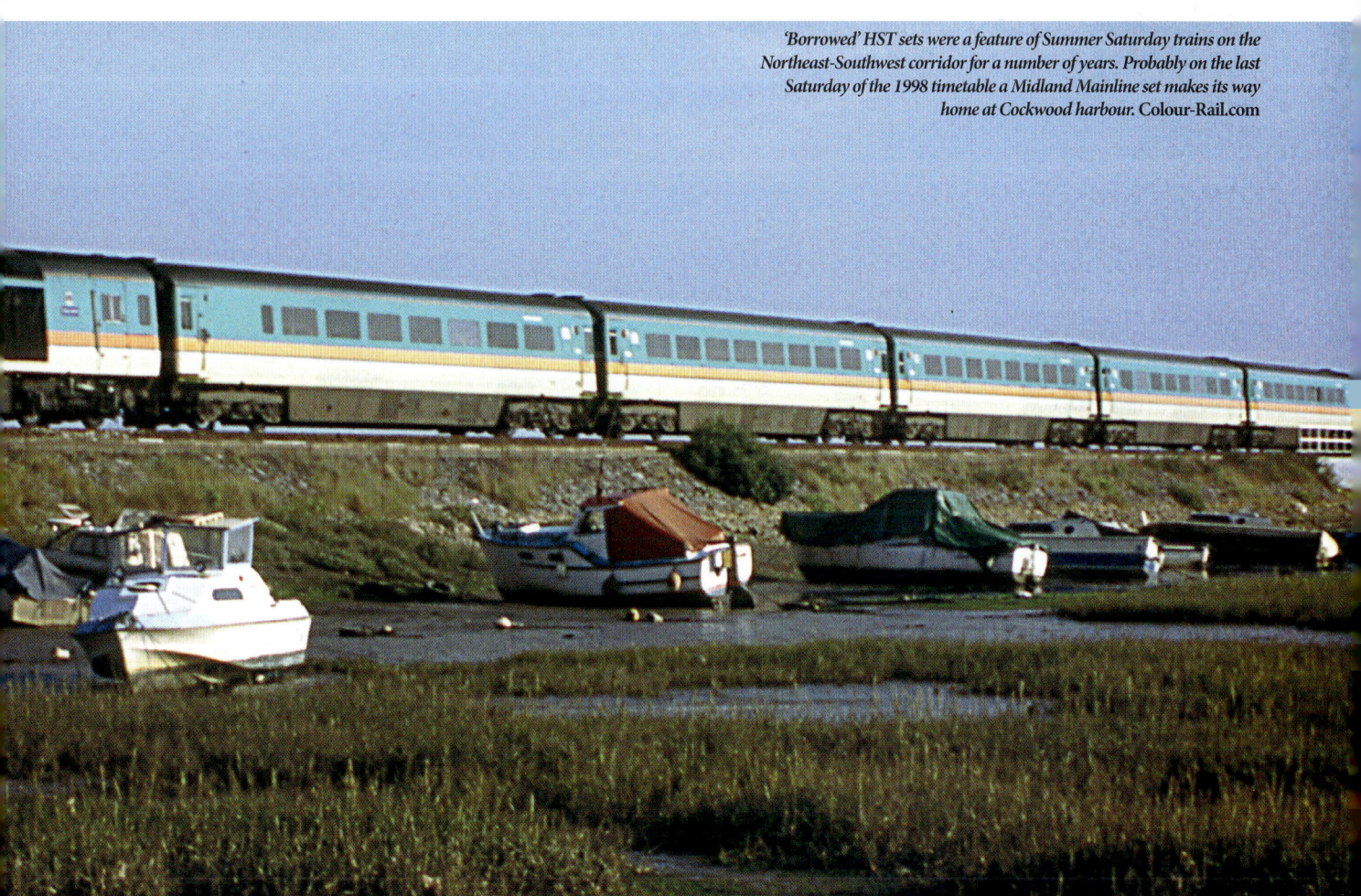

'Borrowed' HST sets were a feature of Summer Saturday trains on the Northeast-Southwest corridor for a number of years. Probably on the last Saturday of the 1998 timetable a Midland Mainline set makes its way home at Cockwood harbour. Colour-Rail.com

The only class 33 to carry EWS colours was 33030, thought to have been repainted for open day duties. So adorned it was recorded at Old Oak Common on 29 August. D Pye/Colour-Rail.com

on June 7 three Virgin sets required help, this being provided by 37701 on two journeys and 37025 on the third. 37701 had also been in passenger action the previous day when it had arrived at Bristol Temple Meads double-heading with 47840 on the 08.40 Penzance-Manchester service. The summer timetable also saw the use of 'foreign' HST sets on Saturday extras with both Midland Mainline and GNER sets working through to the West Country. These were now readily identifiable due to their owner specific liveries.

What turned out to be a very premature railtour called The Long Goodbye ran on January 3 to commemorate the supposed last use in passenger service of a Class 31. It would also have been the final run of any Type 2 diesel on passenger duties. Starting at Blackpool, the tour covered many lines in the north and got as far south as Birmingham New Street. The absence of 31s on passenger duties did not last long as with the advent of the summer timetable they found sporadic employment on, for example, the 10.40 Edinburgh-Bournemouth from New Street.

There appeared to be both a growing variety of test trains accompanied by increased useage with a Track Recording train and a Track Inspection train as well as a Structure Gauging train. All of these ran under the Serco banner and in addition there were a number of trains made up of former DMUs. Where locos were required they were generally hired from EWS.

A potentially serious incident occurred on June 16 when one carriage of the 17.30 Kings Cross-Edinburgh service formed of a Class 91 and Mk IV set

A record for steam haulage was set at Merehead when 9Fs 92203/12 worked in tandem to move a train weighing in at 2000 tonne. They had worked as a pair before at the Great Central Railway but a six coach passenger train tipped the scales at not much more than a tenth of the weight of the one at Merehead. P Chancellor/Colour-Rail

1998

A green painted Duchess had not been seen in action for nearly thirty five years but just before its boiler ticket ran out 46229 Duchess of Hamilton *ran in that guise at the East Lancs Railway and is seen at Burrs on January 30.* P Chancellor/Colour-Rail

became derailed due to a broken wheel, leading to the immediate withdrawal of all Mk IV sets which of course had an immediate impact on East Coast services. After one day, sets were allowed to return to use but with a maximum speed of 80mph which lasted until June 22. High-speed trains maintained some services but many were cancelled though some Class 317 EMUs, plus the three West Yorkshire 321s 321901-3, were hired in and worked from Leeds to Kings Cross – with one reported to have achieved 112mph down Stoke bank.

It was said that freight traffic was buoyant but it generally seemed to be at lower levels than in the past. Over two comparable Saturdays in 1993 and 1998 freight noted at Grantshouse saw the following: 1993 seven trains of which five were coal MGRs one carried pipes and the other was a Willesden Aberdeen van train. These employed between them seven Class 37s, one 47 and three 56s. In 1998 five trains ran of which two were coal, and one each of pipes, steel and Alcan powder tanks employing three class 60s and one each from classes 37 and 56.

The end of a rather brief era but one close to the hearts of many modern traction enthusiasts saw Tinsley depot close on April 4. Its proactive approach to 'breaking the rules' particularly around the naming of is locomotives and turning out depot favourites in liveries that did not conform with corporate instructions set them even to challenge the reputation of Stratford depot for such activities.

EWS gained the contract from Virgin for supplying motive power for the Scotrail sleeper trains

95

leading to the reversion of some Class 90/1 to 90/0 and 110mph running capability. EWS also leased nominally preserved 86101/2.

The era of Eddie Stobart, the Carlisle based haulier, putting freight on rail began on March 30 with trial running between Daventry International Rail Freight Terminal and Hunterston with DRS providing the motive power in the shape of 20306 plus 37611.

Having got through a Great British Winter almost unscathed rail services across the Midlands were severely disrupted from 9-11 April by flooding which closed a number of routes with trains that did get through running up to eight hours late. More flooding at the end of October caused further landslips and extensive delays across much of the system.

The Central Wales line was again used for freight services on May 4 due to a derailment at Cardiff which blocked the route of the Port Talbot to Llanwern trains with these reversing at Craven Arms to reach their destination. Meanwhile solar panels came to some stations on the line to generate electricity for lighting.

The preserved Class 201 DEMU spread its wings to pastures new when it was hired to provide services between Norwich, Great Yarmouth and Lowestoft from July 20. Another blurring of network and heritage sectors saw trains of military equipment running to Wymondham where they moved onto the Mid-Norfolk Railway for deliver to East Dereham.

What was probably the first public appearance of 66001 occurred on June 28 when an open day at Merehead celebrated the 75th anniversary of the formation of Yeoman. As well as most of the Yeoman fleet, 59201 attended along with 33116, 37416, 56103 58050 and 73136. Also appearing were D821 and D1010 along with two Cl 9Fs 92203/12 which double-headed on what were thought to be 2000 tonne trains. 60037/52 brought special trains to Cranmore from Westbury.

The Class 66 'invasion' got under way in August with the arrival of 66003-5, with 66002 being retained in Canada for ongoing testing. These plus 66001 and a host of other locos were to be seen at an open day held at Toton on August 29-30. A number of heritage diesels plus two steam engines were also to be seen. Some locos were repainted specially for the event including 33030 which became the only 33 to carry EWS livery. Another consignment of 66s, 66006-11, arrived in October.

Having closed the shed at Wigan Springs Branch, EWS resuscitated the site by setting up a Central Dismantling and Recovery Centre there which would be used to remove useful parts from locomotives before they were sent for cutting up. Among the first arrivals were 31242, 31459, 47004/16/51, 47210/81, 47467 and 47522/3.

A major landslip on the Settle & Carlisle line at Little Salkeld in July closed the down line. Single line working was in force during repairs which were expected to last until at least October. Another landslip, this time at Lockerbie on July 31, blocked the line and some trains were diverted via the Glasgow & South Western line via Dumfries – achieved by hired pairs of DRS Class 20s. Each train retained its electric locomotive which in the case of one Euston-Glasgow service saw 90024, 87024 plus 20303/4 all coupled for the run to Glasgow. Some services from Edinburgh ran to Carlisle via Newcastle.

The mayors of Chester, Shrewsbury, Oswestry and Wrexham were jilted on October 18 when their party attended Chester station for the naming of a Class 47 as *Spirit of Chester*. The loco failed to turn up for its special day said to be 'required elsewhere'.

Heritage

In signing a subsequently long-standing deal, Southern Locomotives, which owned Standard 4MTs 80078 and 80104 plus a number of Bulleid Pacifics, agreed a supply, running and maintenance deal with the Swanage Railway.

The Bluebell Railway recreated the line's closing train

J27 65894 did not stray from its North Yorkshire Moors home too often but it was loaned to the Yorkshire Dales Railway in 1998 and is seen working a freight train at Bolton Abbey. Colour-Rail.com

1998

run 40 years earlier on March 14/15 by renumbering visiting Standard 4MT from 80080 to 80154 and pairing it with an appropriate single carriage.

The 46229 *Duchess of Hamilton* spent the majority of its time as a restored working engine in BR maroon livery but shortly before the expiry of its boiler certificate whilst working at the East Lancs Railway it was repainted in BR green with the first crest. It retired on March 21. It was repainted back to maroon before return to the National Railway Museum where it was announced that the engine would be returned to streamlined condition, but still with the intention that it would run on the main line. Buckley Wells works run by Riley Engineering was undertaking a large number of contracts for the heritage industry with work under way on 34067 *Tangmere* and 71000 *Duke of Gloucester* with the boilers present from 6201, 7822 and Lancashire and Yorkshire Railway (L&Y) 0-6-0ST 11456.

A preservation scene debutant in the year was Battle of Britain 34081 92 Squadron. Its Malachite Green livery made it stand out from the crowd. On June 21 it was used to recreate a banana train at the Nene Valley Railway. P Chancellor/Colour-Rail.com

The Gloucester-Warwickshire Railway opened a second platform at Winchcombe in late March and the footbridge at Toddington was also brought into use. 2-8-0T 4277 arrived for use on the line.

Under the project name 'Bodiam 2000' the Kent & East Sussex Railway started work on its three-and-a-half mile extension from Northiam to Bodiam. Its first task was to clear vegetation.

The Mid-Norfolk Railway signed an agreement with Railtrack to purchase the line from Wymondham to Dereham plus the station and buildings at Dereham and associated land at a cost of £1m. The County School site also came under the jurisdiction of the railway.

The Keighley & Worth Valley Railway celebrated 30 years of service on September 19/20.

With the relaxation of laws concerning wedding venues a number of heritage lines offered locations where these could take place and the Midland Railway Centre claimed to host the first wedding ceremony held in a signal box, this taking place on August 29.

V2 60800 *Green Arrow* returned to steam for main line duties in August.

The Yorkshire Dales Railway had recently completed its restoration and opening of Bolton Abbey station and marked the occasion with the hire of J27 65894.

Work was scheduled to start in November on the construction of the Swindon Heritage Centre at an estimated cost of £11m.

A new engine on the heritage seen was Battle of Britain 34081 *92 Squadron* which entered service at the Nene Valley Railway in mid-year and carried Malachite green livery but with its BR number. It quickly made an appearance at the Bluebell Railway being seen in action on October 25.

The use of the Severn Valley Railway's direct link to the network facilitated the first ever visit of an HST to Bridgnorth when a railtour from Exeter brought power cars 43027 and 43174 plus a standard set to the Shropshire town. ■

The Ivory and Green livery of Great Western Trains did not last long as the company was sold to First Group. The new company used similar colours and added gold and a large First logo. High-speed train power car 43133 was an early recipient seen at Oxford on June 17. T. Owen

1999

£2bn UPGRADES FOR SCOTLAND

The Channel Tunnel rail link project was rescued by government intervention forming a public/private partnership between Railtrack and London & Continental Railways. The line was now to be built in two parts with the brake at Fawkham Junction with Waterloo continuing as a terminus when the Folkestone-Fawkham section was completed. Upon completion of phase one Railtrack would purchase it. Railtrack would operate the line and levy charges on Eurostar for its use. Eurostar UK would continue to be owned by LCR but the trains would be operated by a consortium of National Express, British Airways and the French and Belgian railways.

With repainting recently completed on all of its high-speed train (HST) power cars and most of the associated trailers in Great Western livery a new livery was noted. It was applied to set LA19, which retained the dark green but replaced most of the Ivory with green and gold bands, and a new logo including the title Great Western and the First Group symbol.

A whole raft of projects to enhance rail freight operations were cited by Railtrack. Many were simply exploratory and few came to fruition although at least one struggles on today – completion of the reopening of the Portishead branch.

Expenditure of £0.5m was authorised on a comprehensive study concerning the feasibility of reopening the Waverley line for passengers from Edinburgh to Galashiels and Longtown-Riccarton for freight. The report, issued late in the year, supported the passenger link proposal with an estimated cost of £35m. A £2bn package of improvements in Scotland were announced by Railtrack. These included the construction of a three-mile electrified line from Haughhead Junction to Hamilton and Larkhall with new stations at Chatelherault, Merryton and Larkhall. Double track was to be re-instated between Barrhead and Kilmarnock.

New Royal Mail terminals were still be constructed at this time with a start being made on one at Bristol Parkway in February. Deputy Prime Minister John Prescott chaired a rail summit where various commitments were made such as investment in more new rolling stock to ensure that half of the total fleet would consist of new or refurbished vehicles by 2002, £39m was to be spent on passenger security measures and a similar amount on customer information systems so that by the end of 2000 every station would have some form of customer communication system. Intentions to re-negotiate some franchises to give improved services were also mooted; setting up a national passenger survey consultation to produce better measures for assessing industry performance and funds for setting up Rail Passenger Partnerships.

Connex South East mounted an attack on Railtrack for failing to complete a £400m scheme started by BR to extend platforms to take 12-car trains. A number remained awaiting attention restricting formations to 10-cars with current plans suggesting that the work would not be complete until 2006.

Planning consent was granted for the construction of Warwick Parkway station roughly halfway between Warwick and Hatton.

The first section of the Jubilee Line extension opened on May 14, this being from North Greenwich to Stratford and was further extended to Bermondsey on September 17, the full line being completed on November 20. As predicted, the Midlands Metro failed to open in January with April then being suggested, with penalties to be paid by the construction and operating consortium reaching £3m by that time. In reality, it was May 30 before services ran between Birmingham Snow Hill and Wolverhampton. Services ran every ten minutes, improving to six minutes by the end of July. The full line journey time was 35mins with 21 stops. Two trams were involved in collisions with cars in Wolverhampton in the first two weeks. The Manchester tram service was extended to serve Piccadilly-Broadway from December 6. The Docklands system had also opened another extension, this being to Lewisham on November 20. The Croydon Tramlink system failed to open as planned in 1999.

The Railways Bill received its first reading in Parliament on July 7 to formalise the role of the new Strategic Rail Authority. A new initiative that patently failed was the establishment of a Commission for Integrated Transport which, as its title suggested, was aimed at getting the rail and bus industries to work together on timetabling and facilities. The Government's new Rail Safety Regulations were also issued. The major requirement brought forward the date for all Mk I rolling stock to be removed to the end of 2004. The Train Protection and Warning System (TPWS) would be required to be installed throughout the network by the end of 2003.

1999

The Midland Metro line from Wolverhampton to Birmingham Snow Hill finally opened at the end of May. Just two weeks later unit 08 was photographed at the Snow Hill terminus. Owen/Colour-Rail.com

Forty people died and 160 more were injured when the most serious rail accident in years occurred at Ladbroke Grove on October 5 when the 08.06 Thames Trains service from Paddington to Bedwyn, worked by 165115, collided with the 06.03 Cheltenham-Paddington HST. Two cars off the 165 were almost destroyed as was HST power car 43011 and coach 41042 was gutted by fire which spread to some other carriages. As a result of the accident Paddington station was closed for 15 days. The nominal cause was the Thames Train passing a signal at danger. The subsequent investigation, which took many months, revealed the specified signal had been passed at danger before because in certain lighting conditions it was very difficult to sight. The signal had been installed during recent track layout changes at Paddington. Driver training issues at Govia, operators of the Class 165 were also highlighted as the driver concerned had only just been passed out. What would have been an almost unreported incident in other circumstances saw another 'passed signal at danger' incident make the national headlines on October 18 when the 17.52 Victoria-Hastings service departed from Lewes against a red signal colliding with empty coach stock (ECS) after a short distance. Fortunately, few injuries resulted but it focused attention on such dangers.

Another item to make press headlines was the arrest of the person controlling Sturry signal box on drug charges. Billed as 'one of the busiest signal boxes on the network' the truth was that the only function of the box was to control the barriers over the A28 road crossing and pull of the associated home signal with the line having an hourly service in each direction.

A pledge at the Tory party conference in 1990 was that Crossrail would be built but ten years later, the project appeared to be moribund. However, one contender for the post of London Mayor suggested that it should be revived and could be open by 2009.

The pace of new station openings faltered in the year but Luton Airport link was opened on November 22.

An end to smoking accommodations on trains moved a step closer in December when First Great Western banned it on all services. It must have been confusing for those wishing to smoke with there being no clear policy across all providers although some had been 'smoke-free' for years.

Cancellations due to lack of staff appeared to be escalating around the country, this being exacerbated on South West Trains where drivers were refusing to work rest days. A statement from the train drivers' union ASLEF advised ➤

The proposal to return trains to the Waverley route as far as Galashiels was gaining traction. Unfortunately the modern station at Galashiels was unlikely to emulate the well-tended facilities found there in the 1960s. Colour-Rail.com

A new station opened at Luton Airport Parkway, one of the largest new constructions on the network. It is seen here soon after the first trains called. B Perryman/Colour-Rail.com

it did not consider the move to be 'industrial action' but it was connected to a claim for a shorter working week which would lead to strike action in the new year.

Stock Changes

For the first time in a number of years locomotive deliveries exceeded 100 with 66002/45-153/6-78 all being delivered. What appeared to be the first effects of these arrivals was that a number of locos were withdrawn from Classes 31, 47 and 73 in January. All of the 66s were nominally allocated to Toton but were soon to be found on many parts of the system. In February the pace of withdrawals quickened with just eight Class 31s being in traffic and a fair number of 47s also going. In addition, Class 37 came under fire for the first time with eight examples condemned. A number of these were subsequently offered for sale. Another ten were added to the sales list in May, this despite the fact that EWS were said to be negotiating a contract with SNCF to send up to forty class members to France for use on the construction of a new TGV line. It did not take long for the first 37s to cross the channel with 37133, 37515 and 37672 being reported as being in France by the end of June. Twenty-four Class 31s were offered for sale in June. The effects of the Class 66 invasions were also to be seen on the Type 5 motive power fleet where a number of Class 56s were put to store. It was also advised that a number of Class 58s due for overhaul would be stored temporarily to defer the cost of that work, the first being 58017 and it was joined by 58022 the next month. 66002 arrived in April along with the highest numbered example seen at that time, 66105. Two members of the class were seen at Inverness on April 24 being 66043/60. Although things could change rapidly by May the use of Class 56s west of Newport had reduced to just two duties whereas at one time up to ten might have been seen with in the past a number being allocated to Canton.

Freightliner announced its intention to join the '66 club' and placed an order for five locomotives for almost instant delivery, this quickly being upped to a total of 20 and 66501/2 arrived in July and like their EWS counterparts entered revenue earning service almost immediately with 66502 working an Ipswich- Birmingham freightliner on July 21. Meanwhile it sold 57001-6 to Porterbrook and then took them back on lease.

Trains hauled by Class 66s rapidly spread throughout the country with two examples noted at Inverness and it was not long before they penetrated even further north on intermodal duties and photographed when 66110 was seen at Helmsdale in 2001. M Thurlow/Colour-Rail.com

100 *Britain's Railways in the 1990s*

1999

A new diesel unit servicing facility opened at Nottingham under the control of Central Trains. This would reduce the need to work units to Tyseley for routine maintenance.

The demise of the Class 141 units appeared imminent with all having been stored prior to 141118 being converted to a weed killing unit. Subsequently four units were offered for sale while the balance were to be returned to the lessor off lease.

Brush at Loughborough seemed to be continuing its rise as a locomotive repair works with twenty six locos present on January 28 including three from the heritage sector.

The first Class 334 unit arrived in Glasgow on August 2. These were intended to work services on the Ayrshire lines currently covered by 318s, the latter then to replace the remaining 303s around Glasgow and the 305s on the Edinburgh-North Berwick line.

Class 170/1 units started to appear in January with two examples being noted at St Pancras. Plans for delivery of the class suggested that they might not appear in set number order with 170/2 appearing before all of 170/1 were completed then some 170/5 before the arrival of 170/4. Indeed 170/5 170502 was seen in service from Derby to Matlock on July 26.

Chiltern announced an order for ten additional Class 168 driving cars with the intention of making up a total of ten three car units by reducing 168001-5 to that formation.

The first two Class 460 Gatwick Express units had been noted on delivery in May as was the first Class 357.

The almost continuous need to hire in at least one Class 90 for East Coast operations in the end resulted in 90024 being painted in Great North Eastern Railways livery but it did not carry GNER branding.

'Enemies within' seemed to have put paid to the hire and use of D9000 for either thunderbird or scheduled services when Railtrack issued an edict to Anglia banning such use on the grounds of safety as it 'inhibited incremental safety improvements'. The fact that a considerable number of diesels built to the same safety standards as D9000 were still active on the network seemed to have escaped its attention. The edict also appeared not to be enforced when Virgin advised that the loco would again work a Ramsgate-Birmingham duty on summer Saturdays. Another heritage diesel on mainline duties was Class 46 D172 which was hired by Freightliner to work a service from Crewe to Seaforth after a number of locos became stranded at Basford Hall due to a derailment.

The end was in sight for the use of Class 141s on the network with all but one in store. The escapee was the former 141118 which was converted for special duties operated by Serco and is seen in 1999. Colour-Rail.com

Class 170 units were being noted across the country with 170/2 in East Anglia and 170/4 in Scotland while the 170/1 variety was in action on the Midland mainline with 170101 recorded at Wistow on May 12. Edward Ward/Colour-Rail.com

In the course of delivery were the Class 460s for use on Gatwick Express duties. They left the works before full application of the livery and required the distinctive nose fairing to be removed to facilitate coupling to the barrier vehicle. 46002 was noted at Reading on April 12. Colour-Rail.com

Britain's Railways in the 1990s

In August EWS reorganised its motive power fleet again with shunter maintenance concentrated on Immingham, Toton, Eastleigh, Allerton, Bescot and Motherwell. At the same time many stored locos moved to 'withdrawn' status including a number of 56s and 58012/27/34. Despite many Class 56s going to store, 56006 appeared repainted from Loadhaul livery to the original BR blue.

A programme of (re) naming all of the GNER Class 91s got underway.

Connex South Eastern received its first Class 375 electric multiple unit (EMU), 375601 in August., A shock to some saw the emergence of 'preserved' Deltic 9016 in purple Porterbrook livery who funded much of its overhaul carried out at Brush Loughborough. The work included the fitting of modern light clusters on each end.

When announcing more information about its new trains being built by Bombardier the marketing name Virgin Voyagers was launched, the order being for both conventional and tilting versions of the diesel electric multiple units (DEMUs). More information was also forthcoming about the electric units which at the time were either to be of 8 or nine cars these being built by Alstom/Fiat Ferrovia and were to be known as Pendelinos.

The latest arrival at Newport docks, this time from Spain was the first of an order for thirty locomotives for EWS designated as Class 67, the delivery being of 67003 on October 6. It was quickly moved to Canton depot.

A further class to be released from works just before the year end was the initial delivery of 175s for First Northwest. The first broke new ground in that 175001 was based on the Severn Valley Railway over which trials were conducted. A 'temporary tent' was put up at Kidderminster to facilitate this, it surviving for a number of years after the 175 had departed.

As planned Eurostar regional and night services looked as if they were never going to happen, GNER announced it had concluded an agreement to hire Class 373 units to work nine trains from Kings Cross to York starting with the 2000 summer timetable.

Services

Anglia was promoting suggested new services with initially trains from Ipswich to Basingstoke these employing its new 170/2 units. The first of these was used at the end of June but initial duties saw them on Norwich-Liverpool Street trains. Unsurprisingly, as they ran generally in four- or six-car formation there was frequent overcrowding as the trains worked by the electric

The continuance of the loan of a Class 90 for East Coast duties led to 90024 being repainted in GNER livery but without the application of the GNER branding. It was noted at Edinburgh Waverley. A Silverwood/Colour-Rail.com

It might have been thought that privatisation might see the final demise of BR blue but various operators revived heritage liveries with 56006 being turned out in blue as found at Rugby in its 'new' colours. B Perryman/Colour-Rail.com

Porterbrook sponsored the revival and restoration of Deltic 9016. In return the engine carried their purple and white colours when seen at York. Colour-Rail.com

Britain's Railways in the 1990s

1999

locos had up to 11 carriages which were also frequently full.

First Great Western re-introduced car carriers to the passenger network in the south west with two vans added to the Paddington-Penzance Night Riviera service from July 28.

Freight traffic at the end of 1998/start of 1999 was 16% up on the same period the previous year and EWS announced a number of new services to reduce through journey times. Freightliner was voted best Freight Operator for the second consecutive year end improved its on-time record from 92 to 96%.

Plans to upgrade services from Nottingham to St Pancras were declared with two per hour in each direction, an express service provided by an HST and a 'stopper' worked by one of the new Class 170 units.

Scotrail 170401 was displayed at Adtranz Derby on August 26 and along with others was soon employed on the Glasgow-Edinburgh express duty, which now operated every 15 minutes.

Operations

A new ScotRail livery was launched with bands of green, red and purple on a white base as seen on 158703/5/6/8 in February.

Proving that nothing seems to be 'for ever' on the rail system, the reported demise of heritage diesel multiple units (DMUs) at Sheffield in the end was very premature with them recently finding regular employment on duties from Manchester via the Hope Valley route.

The use of Class 59s on South Wales steel ore duties which had seen two in regular use for some time came to an end due to an upturn in the aggregates business. They were substituted on some occasions by the ex-National Power 59/2s which had been integrated into the EWS fleet. However their duties in South Wales did not last long with Class 60s in charge by August.

Virgin Trains contracted Alstom to carry out all of its motive power maintenance on the West Coast route which led to another outbreak of sign replacements at the depots which were rebadged as West Coast Traincare Systems.

On June 23 a serious accident occurred at Winsford when, fortunately, an empty Class 142 unit was hit at around 50mph by a service from Euston headed by 87027. Twenty-seven people on the Euston service were injured and 142008 was written off. The impact moved the bodywork three feet forward on the chassis.

Testing of Class 92s took them as far north as Newcastle in June with 92013/34 spotted at Tyne Yard on June 22. The class was finally cleared for use in service north of Wembley in August

Possibly the first use of a Class 66 on a scheduled passenger duty occurred on January 19 when 66016 was used to rescue the 06.48 Shrewsbury-Euston near Telford and the 66 took the train as far as Wolverhampton. However 66016's crown was short-lived as later the same day 66035 was similarly employed from Bromsgrove to Birmingham New Street.

The first steam special organised by West Coast Railways other than the West Highland trains saw 5972 *Olton Hall* of *Harry Potter* fame run to Carlisle from Carnforth. All did not go well with problems providing water at Carlisle and the engine fouling the platform at Citadel station.

Class 31s belonging to Fragonset returned to front line passenger duties taking over duties on the

The Class 66s were dubbed 'sheds' but the Class 67s seemed to defy description although 'unicorn' was applied by some due to the single roof-mounted light. Attractive they were not. 67003, the first to be delivered, ventured on to the restored Kingswear line. R Barnes Collection/Colour-Rail.com

Soon after delivery the first Class 175 unit 175001 was sent to the Severn Valley Railway for operational testing. It spent much of its non-working time in a specially provided 'tent' but also undertook a number of test runs and was seen in the Kidderminster station area. P Chancellor/Colour-Rail.com

Passengers on the Bedford-Bletchley line enjoyed exotic stock and locomotives when, due to a shortage of DMUs, Fragonset provided the trains and 31452/68 were noted at Ridgemont on May 1. Colour-Rail.com

Bletchley-Bedford branch in top and tail mode from March 29 with two Riviera Trains carriages sandwiched between them.

Fragonset started moving its operational base from Tyseley to Derby RTC yard in August.

A temporary station was built on the Whitehall curve at Leeds, this seeing its first trains on September 26. The station was only in use by overnight trains to Manchester Airport on Tuesdays to Sundays when Leeds station was closed overnight for rebuilding.

The Gospel Oak-Barking line saw its Class 117 DMUs replaced on one of the duties by 31468 and 31601 topping and tailing hauled stock on July 15. Next in use were revived 33s 33103/8 with one of them working 4TC 417 although it now only comprised of three coaches. The eventual plan was for Class 150s to work the line.

A rare movement of nuclear fuel by rail on July 19 saw a shipment from Sellafield to Barrow docks for export to Japan. The train carrying the shipment was preceded by a line inspection train which included a carriage full of 'important personnel'. The train comprised a carriage full of policemen, who were also stationed at various crossings, and the journey was shadowed by a police helicopter.

On August 12, an eclipse of the sun – in totality in parts of Cornwall - led to many special trains running from as far away as Scotland to the county. Most used hauled stock with a number of the trains being worked throughout by Class 66s but 37405/10 also reached Penzance and the Hastings unit 1001 worked from its namesake through to Buckfastleigh.

A sign of promotional things to come was the vinyl wrapping of a complete Channel Tunnel Class 373 to promote the Beatles film *Yellow Submarine*. Doubtless it was to capitalise on the re-release of the 1966 original and it was certainly very colourful. Sadly, given the length of a 373, it was almost impossible to capture on film in its entirety.

A passenger train again ran on the Weymouth Quay line on May 2, the first since 1995, this being a railtour from Yeovil headed by a Class 73.

Cardiff had for a long time seen special trains provided when Rugby matches were taking place but those for the World Cup Final on November 6 were exceptional when no fewer than when nine Class 47s were recorded along with Deltic D9009, 33103, 37407/8/30 50031/44 and DEMU 1001. A number of extra HSTs ran as well.

Heritage

The first through passenger train from the Mid-Hants Railway onto the national system ran on January 9 when U 31625 worked from Arlesford reaching the delights of such as Kensington Olympia and East Croydon during the day.

A new arrival on the preservation scene was the rebuilt Furness 0-4-0 No. 20 which had been restored at the Marconi shipyard in Barrow, The engine moved to the Lakeside & Haverthwaite Railway for testing and running in.

Heritage lines had traditionally shut down or run a very limited service after the Christmas and New Year festivities but the Great Central Railway ran a winter steam gala with great success and in 1999 it was held on the last

One of the very first units to receive the latest Scotrail livery was 158707, this being applied by August 20 when it was caught on camera arriving at Edinburgh Waverley. Colour-Rail.com

1999

weekend in January and 6990, 7029, 7821 and 92212 were all in use making it very much a GWR event as 92212 had been a Western Region locomotive. The standard timetable was augmented by TPO, ECS and freight trains.

The NYMR had yet to start its regular services to Whitby but five through trains were planned for the summer season and BR drivers were being trained on steam duties on the line during February, A genuine camping coach was brought into use at Goathland.

Some locomotives on heritage lines were recording high annual mileages with 7820 on the West Somerset Railway putting in 10,900 and 80104 at Swanage 10,600.

Having given the Great Western Society notice to quit from Southall shed the Southall Railway Centre emerged as a new tenant to provide facilities to maintain *Flying Scotsman* and associated rolling stock.

One of the smallest engines approved for mainline use was Ivatt 2MT 41312 which gained its mainline certificate in April and for the proving run was involved in collecting stock from the carriage shed at Clapham Junction thus returning to its old haunts.

The unwary number taker may have been confused if visiting the Dales Countryside Museum at Hawes station where he or she could record G5 67345 on static display. However closer inspection might have revealed its true identity of Robert Stephenson & Hawthorne 0-6-0T built in 1955.

Fortunately for some heritage lines 'big plans' did not always come to fruition, one such being a Railtrack statement that it was on target to reopen the Matlock to Buxton line by 2007.

A Heritage Lottery Fund grant of £1.75m was awarded to the Severn Valley Railway in May to construct a carriage storage shed at Kidderminster with a projected construction time of just six months. Its total length spanning four tracks was one fifth of a mile and it could hold 56 carriages.

The full rebuilding of the Welsh Highland Railway now seemed assured with the issuing of a Transport & Works Order for the remaining 22 miles, this in turn releasing a Millenium grant of £4.3m.

At the National Railway Museum the newly rebuilt workshop and warehouse area was officially re-opened with a public viewing area.

A project to build a GWR Grange 'from scratch' started to gather momentum at the Llangollen Railway. Although essentially a new build, due to the GWR practice of standardisation many of the required parts were already available via other preservation projects, the frames and cylinders being the major items needing to be manufactured.

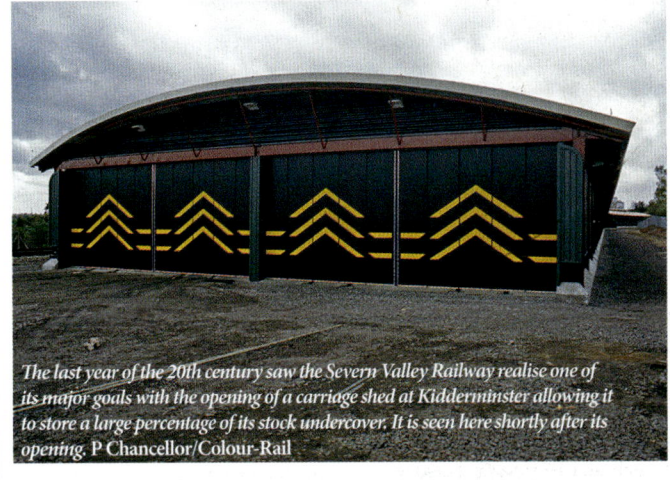

35005 *Canadian Pacific* had a brief career as a mainline certified engine and appeared running in the BR blue livery of the late 1940s and early 1950s although this of course was never carried by a Bulleid pacific in its rebuilt form.

Following the lead of the power stations, and with the closure of collieries supplying good quality steam coal some of the heritage railways started evaluating imported coal with the Llangollen Railway trialling batches from Poland.

A magazine reported that the Keighley & worth Valley Railway appeared to be the only one of 108 that had a female in a senior management position – its president Ann Cryer MP, the former MP for Keighley.

The rarely reported Derwent Valley Railway near York opened its new station at Muton Park on November 28, the building originally being at Wheldrake.

The West Somerset Railway carried 153,832 passengers in 1999 - some 7,000 more than the previous best total recorded in 1997. ■

One of the smallest steam engines to be mainline certified was Ivatt 2MT. Perhaps its most high profile duties saw it used on a Steam on the Met event in May 2000 when it passed through Croxley. Colour-Rail.com

The last year of the 20th century saw the Severn Valley Railway realise one of its major goals with the opening of a carriage shed at Kidderminster allowing it to store a large percentage of its stock undercover. It is seen here shortly after its opening. P Chancellor/Colour-Rail

Merchant Navy 35005 Canadian Pacific enjoyed a brief mainline career and worked a special on January 9 that saw it on the network very close to its heritage base at Loughborough. P Chancellor/Colour-Rail.com

Britain's Railways in the 1990s

Although looking like a preserved loco working on the mainline, Class 25 25322 was still in capital stock although running as D7672. It is seen here on October 27, 1990 working the Rylstone Cowboy tour at Leeds near Holbeck. Colour-Rail.com

1990s RAILTOURS

Railtours for the enthusiast were booming in the early 1990s, the previous decade having seen a major move away from a predominance of tours organised by the railway enthusiast clubs to the setting up of commercially run touring companies. Steam-hauled trains remained as a major part of the market but there was a continued growth in tours using 'exotic' modern traction. With the mainline diesel fleet aging, travellers wanted to 'get in the miles' behind their favourite class before it was too late. Also of note was a change in the rules that allowed the use of 'preserved' locomotives on the mainline although initially there were not many main line certified locomotives available for this work. As the decade progressed the demarcation line between a 'preserved' engine and an old type being hired to run commercial services brought further complications as did the whole privatisation process. For instance should a 'tour' using an high-speed train (HST) running off its normal route and promoted by a company which was a railtour operator actually be called a 'rail tour' as understood by enthusiasts or was it effectively a 'day excursion' which would in years gone by have been organised by BR? The following pages in general concentrate on what might best be described as the 'traditional enthusiast railtours'. Many of the observations recorded below can be found at the excellent sixbellsjunction website.

1990
In excess of 100 tours that could be said were aimed at the enthusiast operated during the year.

The titles employed for the tours seemed very bland compared to some from the 1980s such as the Nose Poker, with the tours basically providing what the headboard proclaimed, thus for instance the Barry Bucketeer, organised by the Growler Group which ran on August 19 went from Crewe via Bristol Parkway and Bridgend to Barry but while there were numerous local shuttles were operated and no fewer than six Class 37s were involved.

The Rylstone Cowboy provided perhaps the only other imaginative train name of the year. Organised by Pathfinder Railtours it ran on October 27 and starting at Swindon ambled via Bristol Parkway, Kidderminster and Macclesfield to Stockport behind 47840 giving way there to 25322 better known as D7672 *Tamworth Castle* this working to Skipton before handing over to a pair of 31s to reach Rylstone.

On May 6, 1990 three trips to the same basic itinerary were run from Walsall to Ironbridge passing through Birmingham New Street on the outward leg where 37101 double-heading with 37298 were recorded on what must have been the third trip if the need for the lights being on is to be believed. D Pye/Colour-Rail.com

106 Britain's Railways in the 1990s

RAILTOURS

The train eventually reached Heysham returning down the West Coast mainline to Birmingham New Street and thence to Swindon worked at various times by the Class 25, 31s and two other Class 47s.

1991
The year saw around a 10% increase in the number of tours operated but was a little more creative in respect of train names such as The Beet Route, The Last Great Mouse Hunt, The Coal Scuttler, The Ayr Restorer, The Beast & Bicycle and the Wye Knot all appearing during the year.

Quite what the connection was between the title, The Beast & Bicycle and the tour is perhaps a little obscure with the train originating at St Pancras and taking a convoluted tour of South Yorkshire and visiting two collieries in the process. It employed pairs of 20s and 27s and ran on September 1 under the Hertfordshire Railtours banner.

The Coal Scuttler was a mammoth tour run by Pathfinder taking 25 and 26 May to complete its journey. It originated at Bristol behind 47818 which worked as far as Warrington with 20131/75 taking over for the run to Carlisle. A tour of Ayrshire, including collieries, followed employing Class 20, 26 and 37 in various combinations to get back to Preston. Though it might have been expected that the train would return to Bristol it then set off to explore parts of Derbyshire behind 56018. Two more 56s, a 58 and two Class 60s were involved before the train returned to Bristol with a total of seventeen locos involved.

1992
The market continued to grow with the tour total exceeding 130 for the year but the inventive marketing suffered a set back with few names to catch the eye

The Plym Rose tour started from Paddington worked by 58027/41 through to Plymouth Friary followed by Class 08 haulage from there to Laira carriage sidings and a pair of 37s thence to Exeter. 56050/1 came on for the final leg back to Paddington via Westbury and Swindon. The same day saw the running of the Tamar Tart which started out from Manchester and employed much of the same motive power and the latter train is seen arriving at Plymouth. J Barnes Collection/Colour-Rail.com

A 'Rail Day' was held at Gloucester on August 4, 1991 which attracted both incoming tours and shuttles operated by 'exotic' motive power with 60048 being so employed on one trip working in from Kemble. D Pye/Colour-Rail.com

On April 25, 1992 a series of short tours under the Lancastrian name were run to the north and west of Manchester and in addition some local workings on timetabled services were worked by special engines with at least nineteen different locos being involved. 58009, seen here at Southport was employed on one trip from there to Manchester via Wigan. G Parry Collection/Colour-Rail.com

but the Cold Turkey, The Bilston Knob and the Hoove-Ring Druid might be worthy of mention. Unsurprisingly the latter employed a pair of Class 50s for much of the day taking them from Derby to South Wales on April 4. It originated at Manchester behind a 47 and employed a 37 for a couple of short sections in South Wales.

As might be expected the Cold Turkey ran after Christmas on December 28 and was organised by A1A Charters and thus featured a pair of Class 31s and running from Stafford they got to Rock Ferry and Wrexham with help from a 37 on three short legs of the tour.

The year was notable for the return of Class 71 E5001 to the mainline it running trips to Bournemouth on both September 12 and 13. Black Cat Railtours used the wonderfully inspired name of the Classic 107 DMU Railtour so there were no prizes for guessing that it was worked by a three car formation ➤

Britain's Railways in the 1990s 107

The Mid Cheshire Rail Users Association ran a one off tour on April 11, 1992 from Manchester via Chester and then the old Western Region route to Didcot, presumably to visit the Great Western Trust site there before returning via Worcester. Worked by 47853 throughout, the photographic interest was in the use of the brightly painted 'Pilkington' set of carriages as seen at Oxford. D Pye/Colour-Rail.com

1994
There was little sign of any slackening in the tour programme despite apparently the country's finances not being in the best of health. In deed the Great Britain appeared again, well almost, as it was now a seven-day tour and was called the Greater Briton and did feature some steam sections. Paddington was again the starting point but only going as far south as Totnes. The steam power in the shape of 68011 was in use for a trip along the South Devon Railway. Moving to Wales day 2 saw steam in use from Bleanau Ffestiniog to Porthmadoc and return. Later in the tour it was the turn of the Strathspey and Brechin Railways to provide steam power with again a 47 and pair of 37s employed on all of the mainline sections. Names attracting attention were the Red Cabbage, The Big E, The Metro Gnome and the Exe Parret.

of said stock spending all day wandering no further than about 30 miles from Edinburgh on June 13.

1993
Not as many tours ran as in the previous year but the total was still well in excess of 100 and with a better selection of weird and wonderful names with the following of particular note: The Kinky Newt, The Paignton Decorator, Coker Coaler, The Par Snip and The Knighton Horse. Something about the tours might be gathered from the names of four of the trains but it was only when the itinerary was viewed for the Kinky Newt that a clue about the name was revealed as 33116 took two 4TC units and a trip to Southampton Docks on October 10 and presumably, with a connection to water the name translated into King Canute.

A noted tour in the year was the Great Briton which ran on October 22-25 so starting the multi day format for which the title became synonymous. However, in 1993 the train was diesel powered throughout and started from Paddington to go to Penzance behind 47823 and perhaps the loco holds the record for the longest run on the same train as it then worked it through to Inverness on day two. Day three was spent visiting Wick and Thurso behind a pair of Class 37s before 47823 resumed its travels working from Inverness to Kingussie and return and then on day four returning the train to London arriving at Kings Cross.

Right **Raildays were frequent events in the early 1990s and one was held at Worcester on May 2, 1993 with incoming tours and local shuttles with one being marketed as the Saucey Slapper which got as far as Long Marston and is seen returning to Worcester at Evesham behind 31106 and 31154. D Pye/Colour-Rail.com**

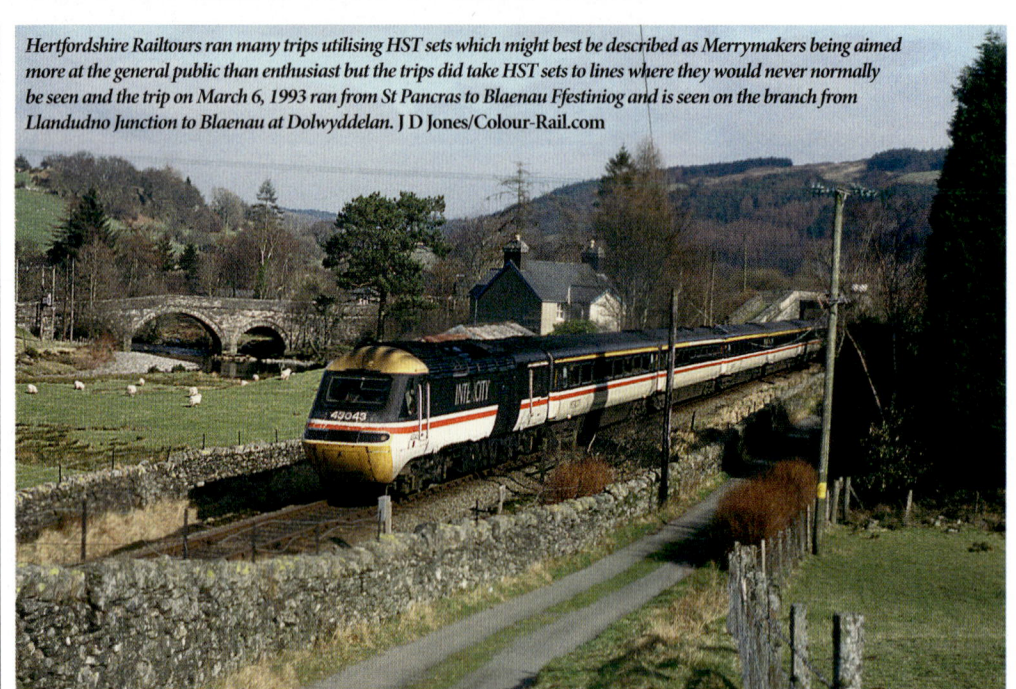

Hertfordshire Railtours ran many trips utilising HST sets which might best be described as Merrymakers being aimed more at the general public than enthusiast but the trips did take HST sets to lines where they would never normally be seen and the trip on March 6, 1993 ran from St Pancras to Blaenau Ffestiniog and is seen on the branch from Llandudno Junction to Blaenau at Dolwyddelan. J D Jones/Colour-Rail.com

108   Britain's Railways in the 1990s

RAILTOURS

A handful of Class 50s remained in BR stock primarily for tour duties and were in frequent demand. The train double-headed by 50007 and 50050 started at Waterloo and ran via Salisbury to Exeter and then through to Penzance returning via the traditional Western region route. They are seen on the outward run at Basingstoke. D Pye/Colour-Rail.com

Above Class 59s were always in demand for tours and 59004 had a run out on May 1, 1994 on The Plym Exe-Cursioner which started from Manchester behind 56125 to Westbury where 59004 took over for a run to Plymouth and is seen at Wellington. It returned the train to Bristol where 56125 returned to action. R Siviter/Colour-Rail.com

Left One of the more creatively named tours was the Exe Parrett commemorating a Monty Python sketch, and ran on October 8, 1994 originating with diesel power from Wolverhampton. It was steam worked by S15 E828 from Bristol via Yeovil to Exeter returning via Taunton with steam as far as Bristol. It briefly halted to regain steam pressure when tackling Honiton bank and is seen here just after the restart. P Chancellor/Colour-Rail.com

The Big E ran from Paddington to Exeter taking participants to the Exeter Railday employing a pair of 20s in one direction and triple headed 37s in the other, this being on May 2. The Red Cabbage ran on February 12 utilising Class 90s to and from North East England with 47626 and 56118 perambulating around points between Teesside and Sunderland.

1995

With privatisation on the horizon 1995 proved to be a much quieter year with the number of tours just about reaching one hundred, but thus still at nearly two every week. Names designed to attract attention were The Prize Porker, The Pheasant Plucker, Tinners and Knockers and the Pigs Trotter.

Britain's Railways in the 1990s

109

Class 47s were often employed on tours, usually as a means of getting the train to 'the interesting bits' of the day out and the Honey Monster tour on July 29, 1995 was no exception as having originated at Paddington it spent much of the day in and around the MoD site at Long Marston. However if a 47 was to be employed then one not usually seen on passenger duties would be best, hence Railfreight Distribution liveried 47348 would fit the bill and was seen at Oxford. D Pye/Colour-Rail.com

Left *A number of tours employed units of one sort or another but did not attract the attention of the photographers as often as loco hauled trains. At least one person took a picture of diesel electric multiple unit (DEMU) 205033 on the Pinner Pieman trip on May 20, 1995 which as might be imagined took a complicated route from London Waterloo to reach Marylebone, Watford (pictured) and Aylesbury during the day. Colour-Rail.com*

Perhaps the significant event of the year, at least as far as steam hauled tours were concerned were the Shap Time Trials series with trains running on 30 September and on October 2 and 3, headed by 6007, 71000 and 46229 with, as the name implied, a timed run up to Shap summit to see which engine would get the best time. These were run and quite strict rules with a maximum speed at the start of the climb not to exceed 60mph and the load being the same for each trip.

The two trains with connections to pigs, The Pigs Trotter and the Prize Porker were run with the same destination in mind. The former ran on October 28 from Leeds and visited the MoD sight at Pigs Bay near Shoeburyness and required five Class 47s to do that while the Prize Porker only ran from Paddington via a complex route around London to reach Essex on March 18, on this occasion needing just two Class 47s.

1996
With a total number of tours struggling to reach even 80 the difficulties of finding a way through the complexities of the new private organisations was evident. Even the inventive names were hard to come by with just The Forceps Nurse on October 18 and the Hail Stone of July 27 attracting attention. November 30 was supposed to be a major highlight for diesel preservation when Deltic D9000 returned to the mainline with a planned Kings Cross-Edinburgh and return scheduled. With the stock being late into Kings Cross the outward run was around 80 minutes late throughout and the return ended in disaster at Berwick with the loco on fire. The only bonus was a rescue by 37702 as far as Newcastle with electric power thence to London. The Great Briton ran gain but basically with the same format as used in 1993 and with no steam power employed.

Once again insight into the tour details was required to decode the Forceps Nurse title which turned out to be a tour from Victoria and visiting three other London stations and never getting further away from the capital than Strood with the train composed of two 4 CEP units.

RAILTOURS

The Paignton Decorator tour on May 25, 1996 employed 56073 throughout on a simple trip to the seaside from Paddington to the expected destination. Travellers missed out however on the rare track into Goodrington carriage sidings where the train was photographed during its layover. R Barnes Collection/Colour-Rail.com

Left *Often seen as not being a railtour, were a number of trains that catered for a small number of passengers on tours around the UK lasting several days with extensive on-train catering and occasionally with sleeping accommodation onboard as well. Regency Rail Cruises was one such organisation and their train employed two Class 37s 37419 and 37406 in the then new English Welsh and Scottish (EW&S), seen at Wellingborough on August 15, 1996. Colour-Rail.com*

Below *Class 33s were rarely seen at Barnt Green on the outskirts of Birmingham but 33116 and 33051 appeared there on May 3, 1997, working The Crewe Cat tour from Eastleigh to Crewe. During the layover at Crewe a secondary trip using 31s, a 56 and 60 operated. R Siviter/Colour-Rail.com*

1997

The year saw a marked recovery in the provision of tours with just over one hundred noted. The run of 'catchy names at the start of the season use among others The Taffy Apple, The Treacle Eater, The Ford Prefect, Tom & Jerry, Even More Bananas and Going Bananas all used before mid-February.

Following its failure at Berwick in November of the previous year D9000 seemed fully revived having a number of outings during the year as well as seeing use on scheduled services.

For steam enthusiasts, the event of the year was on November 22 when steam returned to the Lickey Incline using 2-6-0s 7325 and 42968, both from the Severn Valley Railway and was notable in that the attack on the bank took place in the middle of the

Britain's Railways in the 1990s

111

The Central Wales Navigator tour originated at Sheffield behind 59202 on May 26, 1997, working through to Cardiff. 59204 then took the train via the Central Wales line to Bescot with 59202/4 double-heading the train back to Sheffield. 59202 is seen on the outward leg at Bromsgrove. R Siviter/Colour-Rail.com

The first steam assault on the Lickey incline for some time brought out the photographers in droves. Stanier 2-6-0 2968 and GWR 2-6-0 7325, both Severn Valley Railway based, took on the challenge on November 22, 1997. P Chancellor/Colour-Rail.com

112 Britain's Railways in the 1990s

RAILTOURS

58039/47 provided the rare sight of a member of the class at Weymouth whilst working the Worksop Wessex Wanderer tour on June 27, 1998. This was possibly the first and only through train from Worksop to the Dorset resort and 58039 is seen at its destination. M Thurlow/Colour-Rail.com

Sporting the short-lived Great Western livery HST power car 43009 covers unfamiliar track at Watchet on the West Somerset Railway working a special back to Shrewsbury for Cheshire Railtours on May 9, 1998. M H Yardley/Colour-Rail.com

day unlike many more recent runs which have tended to be either at dusk or in darkness.

Class 33s were by then becoming a bit of a rarity but three were employed on a pair of tours which both ran on April 26, the first setting out around Midnight from Finsbury Park running to Dover and ending up as daylight broke back at Waterloo to form the second tour which went to Salisbury, thence Bristol, down to Southampton, along the south coast and returned to Victoria via Horsham.

1998

The year's tour numbers were similar to those of 1997 but creative names seemed to have deserted the market. It was a year where the number as steam tours seemed to approach those using modern traction. Also just counting the number of tours that were run sometimes gave a false impression of reality with no fewer than seven tours being run in conjunction with an openday held at Toton depot on 29 & 30 of August, named The Sum Toton, Toton Gesture, Totoniser, Toton Eclipse, Toton Recall, and Toton Pole. Motive power was shared by some of the trains but they still managed to employ a Class 37, two 47s, five 58s and two Class 60s.

The year started with a tour entitled The Long Goodbye and it was run to commemorate the end of the use of Brush Type 2s on passenger services. As it turned out this was an extremely premature train as 31s eked out an existence on passenger duties for a number of years, particularly under the Fragonset banner.

Britain's Railways in the 1990s

113

1999

Suddenly railtours were back! The year set a record number at 140-plus recorded. January 2 saw the first tour of the year with a quick return of steam on the Lickey this time with 8F 48773 having a solo run at the bank although with a load of just seven carriages.

Steam tours tended to be concentrated into the cooler months, partly to avoid summer steam bans due to fire risk and the following weekend saw one of the few runs of U-class 31625 on the mainline when it worked the London Explorer from Alton to the capital. On the same day also heading for London was Merchant Navy 35005 running from Crewe to Victoria. Once there, the tour train had an unusual run to Reigate and back behind D9000.

With the railways shutdown for the new year the last tour of the decade ran on December 30th and had motive power appropriate to the coming new age of the railways with 66089 in charge of The Time Lord which ran from Kings Cross to Cleethorpes thence to Barnetby headed by 56114 before 66089 returned it to the capital. ∎

On September 4, 1999 two Class 50s ran from Reading to York at the head of the Hunslet Hoover tour. The by now preserved locos 50031 and D444 are seen crossing the river at Evesham. 60090 worked in top and tail mode from York to Hunslet and Selby with the 50s. R Siviter/Colour-Rail.com

The Red Nose Rambler tour on March 13, 1999 did not cover many miles but did use unusual motive power and reach some rare track. The tour started at Welwyn Garden City using 313056/7 with its first call being at Hornsey EMU depot where the EMUs were towed by both 030179 and 08892 within the depot boundaries. It then continued to the Princes Royal Distribution Centre where this picture was taken before returning to Welwyn. I Thomas/Colour-Rail.com